Reflections on citizenship in a multilingual world

Other titles in the series

Reflections on ICT
edited by Terry Atkinson
REFLECTIONS ON PRACTICE 7

Using technology as part of the process of teaching and learning languages requires careful consideration of purpose and outcome. This book presents a collection of studies which offer a framework for considering how best to ensure effective language learning, based on practitioners' experience and reflections.

Reflections on motivation
edited by Gary Chambers
REFLECTIONS ON PRACTICE 6

The contributions in this book provide a blend of theory and classroom application. They give not only an insight into activities which have succeeded in motivating foreign language learners, but also the rationale behind them – with the aim of providing readers with a template to follow in their attempts to enhance the motivation of their own learners.

Reflections on grammar-implicit language teaching
Margaret Wells
REFLECTIONS ON PRACTICE 5

The action research charted in this book presents first-hand evidence on how teachers and learners responded to two different approaches to teaching grammar – the Grammar-Explicit and Grammar-Implicit methods. Pupils' comments and performance at the end of each year and in their GCSEs provide a valuable insight into learner perceptions and learner progression.

Reflections on the target language
Peter S Neil
REFLECTIONS ON PRACTICE 4

This book examines the use of the TL by ten teachers of German who were preparing their pupils for KS4. It analyses the TL from the teachers' and researchers' standpoint and also looks at the pupils' perceptions of their teachers' use of the TL and of their own language-learning problems.

Reflections on reading: from GCSE to A level
edited by Mike Grenfell
REFLECTIONS ON PRACTICE 2

Three practising teachers consider approaches to reading in a foreign language at intermediate and advanced level in schools and colleges. The first charts the reading habits of a Year 9 class; the other two look at the problems learners face between GCSE and A level and explore strategies which can help to overcome the difficulties.

Series editor: Mike Calvert

Reflections on citizenship in a multilingual world

Edited by Kim Brown and Margot Brown

CiLT | THE NATIONAL CENTRE FOR LANGUAGES

The views expressed in this book are those of the editor and contributors and do not necessarily reflect the views of CILT.

First published 2003
by the Centre for Information on Language Teaching and Research (CILT)
20 Bedfordbury, London WC2N 4LB

ISBN 1 902031 70 9

A catalogue record for this book is available from the British Library

Printed in the United Kingdom by Hobbs the Printers Ltd, Totton, Hampshire SO40 3WX

CILT Publications are available from: **Central Books**, 99 Wallis Rd, London E9 5LN. Tel: 0845 458 9910. Fax: 0845 458 9912. Book trade representation (UK and Ireland): **Broadcast Book Services**, Charter House, 29a London Rd, Croydon CR0 2RE. Tel: 020 8681 8949. Fax: 020 8688 0615.

Contents

Preface

The introduction of citizenship into the secondary curriculum represents an exciting opportunity for language teachers. There are aspects of current practice that we can build on in citizenship teaching and there are new ideas too. The communicative approach, for example, is fundamentally a democratic process and the National Curriculum for Modern Foreign Languages (MFL) offers opportunities for pupils to learn about life in communities around the world and about issues which affect them. Citizenship education brings these two together with the explicit aim of helping young people understand the culturally diverse world in which they are growing up and of preparing them for an active role in their local and global community.

We are delighted to bring together in this book specialists from the language world and from a range of disciplines to explore what citizenship is and what it might mean for language teachers. We argue that modern languages have a central role to play in citizenship education, that there is the potential to build on aspects of good practice already in place but that this is not unproblematic. There are questions to be asked about what we mean by citizenship, there are issues of exclusion and inclusion in current definitions of citizenship and a need for a clear rationale for citizenship education before we can begin to explore this in the context of language teaching and learning.

We hope that the exploration of these issues will hold something for everyone. For teachers, advisers and teacher educators who are just beginning to get to grips with citizenship, we aim to offer a framework for reflection and a starting point for the teaching of citizenship in language lessons. For those who have already begun to think about citizenship and modern languages, we want to ask some challenging questions about definitions and understandings. And we hope that the book will be useful to those more generally involved in citizenship education in schools and other organisations.

The contributors to this book look at different aspects of citizenship education and language learning and teaching. But there are a number of recurrent themes throughout the book. Firstly, there is the shared recognition of the particular contribution that language teachers have to make through their own personal experiences. We discuss this in some detail in the opening chapter. Michael Byram picks up the point in his exploration of *being European* and Jim Anderson and Manju Chaudhuri discuss the important perspective that teachers of community languages bring to citizenship education.

Secondly, there is a general agreement that textbooks currently available and GCSE syllabuses, as they have often been interpreted in the classroom, are narrow in focus and vision. As Michael Byram puts it in one example, many textbooks 'scarcely envisage French as a language spoken outside France'. Jim Anderson and Manju Chaudhuri similarly draw attention to issues often overlooked in MFL lessons 'which tend to trivialise content or message in favour of an emphasis on medium'.

Underlying these observations is an understanding shared by writers in this book of the potential that citizenship education offers MFL in its much broader approach to teaching and learning. The ideas presented in chapters by Margaret Burr or Ian Davies or Jim Anderson and Manju Chaudhuri offer us new ways of working with pupils in secondary and higher education. In the same way, Ann Gregory and her colleagues offer us examples of projects involving primary school pupils in an understanding of citizenship issues. We know from research that pupils in school want to know more about the world they are growing up in and want to learn more about this at school. If levels of motivation in languages have been a cause for concern in the UK, a broader approach and a focus on topics which interest pupils may begin to challenge pupils in their negative views of language learning.

Writers challenge language teachers too in their thinking about language teaching. What do we mean by communicative teaching? This is the question we explore in our first chapter. Why do we correct pupils if they offer us a French word in a German lesson? Michael Byram's promotion of 'plurilingualism' presents an exciting and compelling challenge to current practice. His suggestion that teachers might teach skills for communication of their own language to speakers of other languages is also picked up by Margot Brown in her chapter on asylum seekers and refugees and suggests new thinking about language teaching.

There is a strong element of professional development throughout the book and an acknowledgement of areas that need further work, such as responding to racism in language lessons. Hugh Starkey's and Audrey Osler's chapter is particularly important for the attention they draw to the risk of reinforcing stereotypes in language lessons and for the need for teacher development in this area. Michael Byram also points to this need. Ian Davies shows how, by offering student teachers experience of citizenship issues during their training, we can help to ensure sound citizenship teaching in schools. Througout the book we have included points for reflection, indicated by a tinted strip and the letter 'r' to support and encourage discussion with colleagues of citizenship issues.

We hope that the introductory chapter will encourage teachers to adopt a reflective and questioning approach to definitions and understandings of citizenship. And we hope that the book as a whole provides the stimulus and support you need to take the first steps towards reaffirming the central role of modern languages in the education of young citizens in schools today.

Introduction – Opening the debate on citizenship and modern foreign languages

Kim Brown and Margot Brown

We would like to begin this chapter, as we begin many of our teachers' workshops, with an example. This one is taken from a Spanish teaching pack about Mexico and focuses on the topic of tourism. The activity illustrates what citizenship education might look like in the modern languages classroom and introduces the main points of discussion in this chapter. While the topic of tourism may be familiar enough to language teachers, we think the approach here is different and one not usually associated with language teaching and learning.

Before you read on, take a moment or two to think about the kind of activities which textbooks suggest and the resources you have available to teach tourism. What vocabulary and grammar structures do pupils learn and how do they learn these? What are they asked to do with this new language? Do pupils focus on their own community, for example, by preparing leaflets for their exchange visitors about local facilities, or do they learn about another place? What is the aim of teaching about tourism? It might be helpful to jot down these thoughts at this point or to discuss this with colleagues in your department.

The activity we want to consider is based on a true story of a project for a tourist complex and golf course in the town of Tepoztlán not far from Mexico City.[1] Controversy developed over the appropriate use of land in the area. An international company wanted to buy and build on land partly in the National Park and on ancient burial grounds which were sacred to the local community. The local residents wanted to protect the traditions and beliefs of their ancestors and were also concerned about the environmental damage to their land and water supply incurred by the development and maintenance of the golf greens and tourist centre. Pupils are asked to consider views of people from different groups involved in the controversy. They read statements aloud to each other, discuss them and decide how to group them according to the views expressed. They have to work together and come to a consensus to complete the task successfully. They practise the language they are learning and at the same time learn about the ways in which people can express their views and protect their rights in a democratic society.

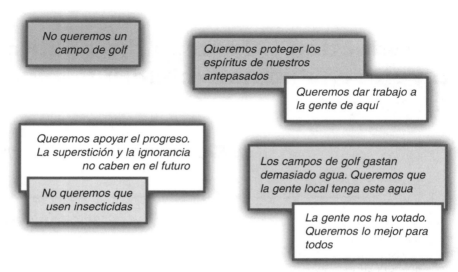

Examples of views expressed in the controversy

This activity contributes to the citizenship curriculum by bringing together tourism, human rights issues and environmental concerns. It raises the question of the appropriateness of using agricultural land to service the tourist industry. While the events described here took place in Mexico, the issue has resonance for many communities in the world, including those speaking languages which are taught in schools in this country.

Some of you may be fortunate to work with colleagues in humanities, for example, where this type of activity will be familiar. You may have tried similar group-work activities with pupils, where they match or sort cards. But to what extent has the explicit aim of raising issues of social justice or human rights been part of language teachers' practice? It is this fundamental aim which distinguishes citizenship teaching from typical language teaching tasks currently available to teachers.

 If you now go back to the notes you made on the resources and activities that you have available to teach tourism, how many involve pupils in the issues around tourism? Do any of the tasks involve group work and discussion and what are pupils asked to discuss?

Firstly, there is the context of a real controversy set in Mexico. We know from research studies (MORI, 1998; 2001) that young people want to know more from their teachers about issues which affect them and young people and their families around the world. They want to know more about environmental concerns, for example, or ethical issues and war and peace studies.

Secondly, as one participant in our workshops with teachers observed, the activity does not impose a single viewpoint on pupils. She felt this was in marked contrast to activities in current textbooks which tend to present pupils with a fixed and uncontroversial perspective on, for example, life in France or tourism in Spain. Many language teaching resources present pupils with a stereotypical view of the world. The focus of activities may be on vocabulary learning or practice of language structure but not usually on issues raised by the resources on which the lesson is based.

It may be thought that this approach is close to the teaching of cultural awareness in language lessons, but again there are important differences. Where many language teaching resources tend to focus on events in the metropolitan country of the language being learned, France, for example, citizenship education takes a broader view and suggests the use of sources of information from other communities speaking this language, such as Martinique or Sénégal. The focus on issues of global significance introduces a still broader approach. French tourists, for example, visit many communities where French may not be spoken but where they encounter human rights issues or environmental campaigns which are familiar to them. In other words, it is by engaging with the issues that interest French people or Spanish people as citizens that we engage with French or Spanish culture: citizenship issues transcend national boundaries. This may be a new way of thinking for some language teachers and marks a clear distinction between current practice and citizenship education.

The events in Tepoztlán had a positive outcome for the local residents in that they prevented the building of the golf course. The National Park and their burial grounds were safe and their water supply was protected. The activity contributes to the citizenship curriculum in the following ways:

- it offers pupils the chance to become informed about issues affecting people in another community in the world;

- it gives them the chance to consider different perspectives and to express their own views;

- it helps pupils learn about the ways in which local communities work and how people can defend their rights;

- it offers them a model of responsible action for change taken by members of a local community in political events which affect them.

The activity helps pupils to develop **knowledge, values** and **skills**. And it is the fact that it makes concrete the concepts which are fundamental to citizenship education that makes it a citizenship activity.

We hope that this example shows how different citizenship teaching is from most current language teaching practice and, at the same time, how much potential there is in current practice to develop a citizenship approach. We now want to consider some of these ideas in more detail.

- Firstly, we want to look at the official definitions of citizenship and to raise some questions of interpretation. We all need to be clear about what citizenship **is** before we can consider how we might teach it in our lessons.

- In the second section we consider the particular contribution that modern language teachers can make to education for citizenship.

- In the third section of this chapter we consider the schemes of work produced by the Qualifications and Curriculum Authority (QCA) and the exemplar units for MFL.

- Finally, we shall look at the question of establishing democratic processes in the language classroom. We hope that our suggestions for the monitoring of lessons and for sharing good practice across subject departments will raise language teachers' awareness of the importance of **process** in pupils' learning.

Citizenship education: definitions and understandings

A FRAMEWORK FOR CITIZENSHIP EDUCATION

So, what is citizenship? Firstly, we need to make a clear distinction between citizenship and education for citizenship. The former involves, for example, legal and political recognition of the rights and responsibilities of individuals in nation states of the world. The latter looks at ways in which teachers can help pupils to develop the knowledge, understanding and skills they need to protect these rights and assume these responsibilities. We live in a diverse, multi-ethnic and multi-lingual society. Our concept of citizenship and how we teach it requires us to engage fully with this. While we are focusing on education for citizenship in this book, with regard to language teaching, we clearly need to ensure that those of us working with young people sufficiently understand citizenship issues ourselves if we are to teach pupils well.

The framework for citizenship education in schools is based on recommendations from the Advisory Group on Citizenship which was set up by the government in 1997 (1998, Qualifications and Curriculum Authority, QCA). The Final report of the Advisory Group is sometimes called the 'Crick report' in reference to Professor (now Sir) Bernard Crick who chaired the Group. In summary, the report sets out the aim and purpose of citizenship education, three strands of citizenship education, and a range of learning outcomes for pupils. The aim and purpose of citizenship education is expressed in the following terms:

> *The purpose of citizenship education in schools and colleges is to make secure and to increase the knowledge, skills and values*

relevant to the nature and practices of participative democracy;
also to enhance the awareness of rights and duties, and the sense
of responsibilities needed for the development of pupils into
active citizens; and in so doing to establish the value to
individuals, schools and society of involvement in the local and
wider community. (1998, QCA, Section 6.6, page 40)

The Advisory Group identified three strands of citizenship which form the basis of the Programme of Study for Citizenship Education in the National Curriculum, **social and moral responsibility, community involvement** and **political literacy**. Learning outcomes for pupils are founded on four essential elements: concepts; values and dispositions; skills and aptitudes; and knowledge and understanding.

The Crick Report formed the basis on which the National Curriculum Orders (DfEE, QCA 1999) were developed. There are some differences in the way in which the two documents structure and describe citizenship education and it is important for teachers to remember that it is the Orders which represent the legal requirement. So that where the Crick report refers to the three strands of citizenship as above, the National Curriculum documentation and the QCA schemes of work which have been developed to support teachers, talk of citizenship education in terms of: **knowledge and understanding about becoming informed citizens; developing skills of enquiry and communication; and developing skills of participation and responsible action**.

It is helpful to think of citizenship education in terms of teaching and learning **about, for and through** citizenship.

 • Teaching **about** citizenship engages pupils in learning about concepts, such as democracy, human rights and equality; about individuals and institutions which support democratic citizenship; about people who are activists and local case studies which exemplify good citizenship; and about citizenship issues such as voting rights in the UK and in other countries.

 • Teaching **for** citizenship describes a skills-based approach. In order to encourage pupils to develop independence of learning and participation skills such as negotiation and compromise, teachers plan lessons with a range of learning needs in mind. Active learning strategies such as collaborative group work are particularly important for citizenship education. The focus is on ensuring smooth and effective learning in a well-managed classroom and on the preparation of pupils for life beyond the classroom.

 • Finally, education **through** citizenship describes pupils' experiences of democratic processes in the course of their schooling, for example, through Schools Councils or through the democratic organisation of their classroom. A reflective and explicit approach to classroom management and to relationships in school can help pupils to engage with the principles of democratic processes.

The introduction of citizenship education in schools places a number of responsibilities on teachers and relies on their clear understanding of concepts such as citizenship and community and responsible action. In the following section we want to raise a number of questions about these concepts which have a direct bearing on teachers' work with pupils. *How do we define ourselves in terms of community? Who is excluded by these definitions of community?* The third question, *What is meant by participation and responsible action?* will be discussed in the final section of this chapter.

HOW DO WE DEFINE OURSELVES IN TERMS OF COMMUNITY?

The challenge for teachers is to help pupils develop and feel a sense of belonging to and responsibility for a number of different communities, local, national and global. There are legal and political definitions, such as belonging to a nation state – *He's German* – or to a political and economic community – *I'm a European* – which are based on the rights or duties of citizens to vote. But what about belonging to an international community? While the Advisory Group acknowledged membership of Europe in their definitions of citizenship, on the basis that Members of the European Parliament are elected representatives, they do not recognise citizenship of an international community in the legal sense and their references to international issues are neither strong nor focused. In the same way, different kinds of communities, such as faith communities or gender communities, or the global community which may have equal or more importance to their members than politically defined communities are not recognised in the current definitions of citizenship that teachers are going to be working with in schools.

There is also the question of diversity within communities. For example, the statement *I'm British* appears to imply a common understanding of belonging to this community. But national and regional communities are not homogenous and within a national community there will be diverse identities such as cultural, religious and ethnic identities to take into account. In other words, this diversity makes even the notion of a national identity contested. Does being French, for example, mean the same thing to someone whose family heritage is African or Arabic as it does to a person whose family heritage has always been rooted in France? This is the kind of question we need to ask ourselves and our pupils in our citizenship teaching.

WHO IS EXCLUDED BY DEFINITIONS OF COMMUNITY?

The notion of belonging to a community reinforces at the same time the situation of those who do not belong. Where citizenship is defined only as voting rights there will always be individuals or groups who are denied the right or who reject the duty and therefore fall outside the narrow definition of citizenship. A simple dictionary definition shows the potential for discrimination that narrow interpretations of citizenship can hold:

A citizen

A member of a state, an enfranchised inhabitant of a country, as opposed to an alien (Shorter Oxford English Dictionary)

Words like **enfranchised** and **alien** underline some of the issues around membership of a community. For example, members of the Traveller community may find themselves excluded from the voting register if they are following their traditional life-style and are unable to register a postal address at the time of an election. Homeless people most certainly find themselves disenfranchised as they have no fixed address and, despite having a very fixed address, residents of prisons or mental institutions have no right to vote. Groups like these within our communities are not only technically disenfranchised but are also among those whose voice is rarely heard, whose experience of living within the community is rarely recognised and whose involvement in community affairs is considered unwelcome. They are also missing from the citizenship curriculum.

For asylum seekers and refugees there are particular ironies around notions of citizenship and citizenship education. They constitute a group who are largely excluded from wider community life and who often experience racism and discrimination but whose children will be included in citizenship lessons in school. Furthermore, the unit in the QCA schemes of work which focuses on racism makes no reference to the people who are affected by it. As recent research suggests, in most schools, teaching about refugee issues 'will be a missed opportunity – missed because there is no **explicit** guidance on how to teach issues of injustice and exclusion, including refugees' (Rutter, 2002).

Governments are usually the bodies which select the criteria by which people are deemed to be citizens of a country. For example, until 1981, you were British if you were born on British soil and it was government legislation that changed that policy. Immigration and nationality laws, brought in by government, are important elements of the legal definition of citizenship. And yet pupils are not encouraged in the citizenship curriculum to discuss questions such as who decides who has the right to be a citizen or issues such as nationality or immigration in the acquisition of British citizenship (Rutter, 2002). While the notion of citizenship clearly carries implications of inclusion and exclusion, the citizenship curriculum does little to encourage the exploration of these issues.

It is for this reason that some educators believe a human rights framework offers a more inclusive definition of citizenship, that is, membership of the human race. By dint of being human, an individual has rights. He or she may not choose to access them or may be denied them, but there are rights which are incontestable and more all-embracing than the right to be a member of a nation state. While human rights issues are included in the definitions of citizenship in the Advisory Report and in the QCA schemes of work, a more inclusive approach might be to suggest that citizenship is part of the much broader notion of human rights. This is an important debate. Teachers need to be aware as they plan their lessons on citizenship that they will be teaching children whose families are denied their right to vote or who are excluded from National Curriculum definitions of citizenship as they stand.

Teachers may wish to consult more broadly. A number of recent reports include recommendations for schools which affect citizenship:

- The Macpherson Report into the death of Stephen Lawrence makes recommendations that require schools to work actively against racial discrimination. Ofsted is also required to ensure that these are implemented.

- The Race Relations (Amendment) Act (2000) requires educational institutions to eliminate unlawful discrimination and to promote equality of opportunity and good race relations. The Commission for Racial Equality offers guidance on this.

- The Human Rights Act, 1998 (which is addressed in a unit of the schemes of work for Key Stage 3) covers education and family life and represents the incorporation of the European Convention on Human Rights into British Law.

- The Report on the Future of Multi-Ethnic Britain (known as the Parekh Report, 2000) offers reflection and guidance on questions of ethnicity and equality in its chapter on Education. It also comments on the links between equality issues and citizenship:

  'Although equal citizenship is essential in developing a common sense of belonging, it is not enough. Citizenship is about status and rights, but belonging is about full acceptance. An individual might enjoy all the rights of citizenship and be formally equal, ... and yet feel that they are not fully accepted ... full acceptance is a deeper notion than inclusion. For a long time there was no legal concept of a British citizen ... even now citizenship is seen in dry, legal terms, and there is little moral or emotional significance in the status of citizen.' (Parekh report, 2000)

These wider, more encompassing pieces of legislation and documentation, while not written specifically for teachers, remind us that citizenship education is part of a broader process promoting equality and social justice. Language teachers have personal experiences of some of these issues and this gives them an important role to play in citizenship teaching. This is the focus of the next section.

Language teachers and citizenship education

Many language teachers will have spent a year abroad as part of their undergraduate degrees. We have the experience of learning another language, of living in a different language-speaking community, and of reflecting on similarities and differences between our home community and the new one. Those teachers who are native speakers of the modern language they teach in the UK will have met similar challenges and rewards.

We will all have experiences of being made to feel welcome by friends and colleagues, but may also have encountered less positive attitudes. Some of us will have encountered mildly irritating stereotyping – *it always rains in England, all Scots live in haunted castles*. But some language teachers will have encountered much more hostile stereotyping than this. For example, German-speaking student teachers in the UK sometimes have to deal with Hitler salutes from pupils as they walk into their classrooms to teach. And some student teachers from Algeria and other French-speaking communities have encountered unacceptable racism in the schools in which they have taught. Community language teachers and many pupils speaking these community languages live with these challenges daily.

Citizenship education calls for the teaching of values, understanding and skills as well as knowledge about life in other communities to help pupils develop a respect for cultural diversity. Language teachers have particular experiences to draw on which give them a vital role to play in the teaching of citizenship in schools. Where teachers of PSHE or history, for example, are being asked to teach citizenship because of the subject they teach, language teachers have much more personal experience of the issues that lie at the heart of citizenship education. Far from suggesting, as some more reluctant teachers might, that citizenship has nothing to do with language teaching, we argue that language teachers have a central role to play.

The introduction of citizenship education offers all teachers the chance to review their current practice. For language teachers, it means the chance to reinstate aspects of language learning, such as cultural awareness and language awareness which have tended to take second place to transactional language teaching. There are places in the citizenship curriculum which encourage language teachers to build on their experiences of diverse cultures in their teaching. The National Curriculum Orders for Citizenship Education **require** teachers to reflect on these things with their pupils.

Exploring the full potential for citizenship education in modern foreign languages

The QCA recognises the challenge of citizenship education and has produced schemes of work and exemplar units in each curriculum subject to support teachers in their planning. But, as we go on to discuss, the provision of citizenship education is not without its problems. The QCA stress that their approach to provision is 'light touch' and suggest a range of options for teachers and curriculum co-ordinators:

The scheme of work is designed to allow teachers to deliver citizenship through a combination of:

- discrete provision for citizenship within separate curriculum time;
- explicit opportunities in a range of other curriculum subjects;

- whole-school and suspended timetable activities; and
- pupils' involvement in the life of the school and wider community.

(QCA, 2001, Teacher's guide, page 3)

But there are difficulties in this reassurance of a light touch. Firstly, there is the difficulty of ensuring a coherent experience for pupils in lessons across the curriculum. Will pupils always be made aware by different teachers that opportunities in their lessons for independent learning or group work tasks are an explicit part of their citizenship education? This requires clear thinking and shared planning on the part of teachers.

Secondly, there is the concern that a 'light touch' approach might lead to over-simplification and tokenism and that citizenship education will be diminished as a result. For example, it is suggested in the QCA exemplar units that pupils can learn about Christmas customs in German- or Spanish-speaking countries and develop an awareness of differences and similarities in cultural traditions (German, Unit 8 *Essen und Feiertage*, Spanish, Unit 2 *La familia y los amigos*). In another example (French, Unit 7 *Les autres pays*) pupils match half-sentences such as *Au Canada on joue au hockey sur glace, Au Québec on parle français*. These activities aim to introduce questions of cultural diversity into language lessons and yet there is no mention of Muslim communities in Germany, for example, or of the indigenous peoples in Canada. The underlying assumption is that these communities are homogenous. The QCA stresses that the examples they give are intended as a starting point, but there is a real risk that activities like these fail to address citizenship issues and fail to engage language pupils and teachers in citizenship education. Far from a 'light touch', we are suggesting that citizenship education is important enough to make an in-depth engagement with the issues worthwhile.

 How can you ensure that your department adopts a sound approach to the teaching of citizenship? Who might you talk to in your school about this?

There **is** scope to address citizenship and human rights issues in the context of GCSE topics. Pupils can learn about rights and responsibilities, for example, through the experiences of children around the world, of poverty or war or of prejudice (see Brown and Brown, 1996; 1998 for further discussion of these ideas). A number of non-governmental organisations, such as ActionAid, are beginning to develop resources for language teachers to support the exploration of issues like these. We are not simply saying that language teachers are good for citizenship but also that citizenship offers new opportunities and fresh beginnings to language teachers and learners too. There are elements of our practice we can develop and new understandings we can gain in talking about citizenship teaching. In the next section we want to look in particular at the teaching of citizenship skills in the languages classroom.

Citizenship skills: some issues of interpretation

COMMUNICATIVE TEACHING: A DEMOCRATIC PROCESS?

Some language teachers tell us they are teaching citizenship already and often cite communicative teaching and active learning as examples. While there are undoubtedly elements of citizenship skills intrinsic in communicative methodology, there are differences too. The message we want to convey here is not to be too hasty – there are exciting strategies for encouraging classroom interactions that language teachers will miss out on if they do not explore citizenship teaching to the full.

Many language classrooms **are** lively, communicative places. In classes we have observed, pupils are encouraged to take the initiative, to greet the teacher in French or Spanish, or to conduct parts of a lesson, such as spelling tests, themselves. There are opportunities for independent learning, group projects and for individual study. But this only goes so far in meeting the requirements of the citizenship curriculum.

Citizenship skills of enquiry and communication, for example, require pupils to 'contribute to group and exploratory class discussions and take part in debates' (Citizenship Programme of Study 2, c). Active learning and group-work tasks which are central to citizenship teaching entail discussion with pupils of the process of their learning as well as the content. They are encouraged to reflect on the role they have played in group tasks, on conflicts they might have experienced and on ways in which they might deal with these another time. Both of these aspects of citizenship teaching represent considerable change for language teachers, including those who already encourage high levels of pupil interaction.

 Citizenship education requires pupils to learn to work together. It might be helpful to monitor classroom interactions or to review departmental policy on teaching in the target language. If your department wants to try some group-work tasks which tackle citizenship issues, it may be necessary to teach pupils the language they need to take part: *Je suis d'accord/pas d'accord; Ich stimme zu/Ich stimme nicht zu; Meiner Meinung nach/Was meinst du?*

In other classrooms we have observed, pupils have a more passive role. Communications tend to be highly structured, teacher-led, question and answer activities. Pupils listen to explanations and instructions, and answer questions but are less often encouraged to ask them. Research and inspection evidence has shown that even when teachers know that their lessons are being monitored to assess the pupils' participation in the target language, it is far outweighed by teacher talking time (Neil, 1997; Dobson, 1998).

In order to teach citizenship effectively, we need to ensure high levels of pupil participation in lessons. We saw how the Spanish activity involved pupils in group work, independent of the teacher, and how the task helped to develop communication skills as pupils exchanged views, took part in negotiation and worked towards consensus. For all language teachers, citizenship education represents a challenge and the chance to reassess the nature of interactions in our classrooms.

WHAT DO WE MEAN BY PARTICIPATION SKILLS AND RESPONSIBLE ACTION?

Participation, as it is understood in the citizenship curriculum, goes beyond spoken interactions in the classroom: it involves pupils in **action** in the different communities to which they belong (see Hart, 1997 for more on this). We saw in the Mexico activity how the tasks helped pupils to understand community action. Language teachers are familiar with activities in the classroom which simulate action that pupils might take in their local community. For example, they might conduct a survey to determine leisure facilities that are needed in their community for young people or they might write letters of protest or support for plans to extend a shopping precinct. The next step is to take the action out of the classroom and into the communities themselves.

One assignment in the *Bengali Manual* (see page 58) asks community language learners to conduct a mini-conference with other Key Stage 4 students. They need to decide on the theme of the conference, its chair and the speakers and the information to go in the conference packs. They need to work within a specified budget to plan the venue, catering, publicity and booking arrangements. They also have to write up a report summarising discussions and decisions and to circulate this to appropriate bodies such as the High Commissions of Bangladesh and India, Bengali-speaking youth groups and to the United Nations. In this way, students experience citizenship through their learning and their participation in the conference. *Manju Chaudhuri*

It might be possible to develop links with work experience programmes between local companies who work and trade in languages other than English and schools. There may be established communities of Italian or Polish speakers, for example, in local towns and villages which pupils could contact and work with. They might stage short plays in the language they are learning or concerts of songs from that country for the elderly in their community at day centres or residential homes. They might be encouraged to compare and contrast the care of the elderly in their own community and that of the partner school they have an exchange with. The important aspect of these suggestions is that pupils learn by doing, they become informed about issues affecting citizens in their communities and others, they develop skills of inquiry and participation and an understanding of how and why to take responsible action about issues in their local community. It is through this involvement at local level that young citizens become engaged in issues of national, international and global significance.

Conclusion

There is continuing concern about levels of motivation in language lessons and a number of pupils leave school without the language skills they need to play a full role in an increasingly globalised and multi-lingual world. The introduction of citizenship is prompting whole school planning and collaboration between teachers across the curriculum. Many of the language teachers at our workshops have not been included in these plans. We hope that this book will support those who are keen to know more and help those who are more sceptical to see the importance of citizenship for modern languages. Young people need languages and they want to learn about issues affecting different language communities around the world. If we are to play our full part in their development as young citizens, we need to look for new ways of teaching languages.

Bibliography

Brown, K. and Brown, M. (1998) ResourceFile 1: *Changing places*. CILT.

Brown (2002) pp138–147 in: Grenfell, M. (ed) *Modern languages across the curriculum*. Routledge Falmer.

DfEE/QCA (1999) *Citizenship: the National Curriculum for England*. QCA.

Dobson, A. (1998) *MFL inspected: reflections on inspection findings 1996–7*. CILT.

The future of multi-ethnic Britain: the Parekh report (2000). Profile Books.

Hart, R. (1997) *Children's participation,* Earthscan Publications.

The Human Rights Act (1998) The Stationery Office.

Macpherson, W. (1999) *The Stephen Lawrence inquiry: report of an inquiry*. Stationery Office.

MORI (1998) *Children's knowledge of global issues – a research study among 11–16 year olds;* Schools survey, 2001 *Young people and citizenship*.

Neil, P. (1997) *Reflections on the target language*. CILT.

QCA (1998) *Education for citizenship and the teaching of democracy in schools: Final report of the Advisory Group on Citizenship*. QCA.

QCA (2000) *Citizenship at Key Stages 3 and 4: initial guidance for schools*. QCA.

QCA (2001) *Citizenship: a scheme of work for Key Stage 3*. QCA.

Race Relations Amendment Act (2000).

Rutter, J. (2002) *Asylum seekers and refugees, modern language teachers and citizenship education* (available from the author, London Metropolitan University).

The shorter Oxford English dictionary (3rd ed) (1973). Clarendon Press.

Vidas Mexicanas (2001) available from Centre for Global Education, York St John College, York.

Notes

1 For a fuller discussion of this activity in the MFL classroom, see Brown (2002) pp138–147 in Grenfell, M. (ed) *Modern languages across the curriculum.* Routledge Falmer.

The resources are part of a Development Education Pack *Vidas Mexicanas* (2001) available from the Centre for Global Education, York St John College, York.

Chapter 1

Teaching languages for democratic citizenship in Europe and beyond

Michael Byram

Michael Byram challenges us to think about language teaching in new ways. How do we respond if a pupil communicates in German in a French lesson, for example? Byram suggests we should be encouraging pupils to work across a number of languages in language lessons. We should be taking up any opportunity to challenge their monolingualism and go beyond stereotypes and prejudice. Language teachers are teachers of values and democratic processes as well as of language skills.

In 1916 the American philosopher of education, John Dewey, proposed a vision of schools as places where young people become participants in a democracy. Democracy for him is not simply a political system but a way of life, an active participation in a society and interaction with other people. This is a crucial element of his concept of progressive education. He then identifies the counter-acting forces of conservative education, the forces which are inimitable to democracy, as those social bodies which seek isolation in and protection of what they have, rather than seeking progress through wider relationships. The first of his examples of conservative forces is the nation-state, and in 1916 nation-states were displaying their isolationism and protectionism on the battlefields of Europe.

By chance, I am writing these pages not far from those battlefields on the first day of the Euro and have just bought my bread in francs, receiving my change in Euros. The symbolism of this would not escape teachers of European languages:

> *We have this island mentality which accounts for an awful lot in our educational system still and in our outlook in general, I think, and our attitude towards the foreigner and also this feeling of superiority towards the rest of Europe.*

The biggest problem we have is trying to encourage our children to feel European, and that is because adults have talked a long time about 'we'll go across the water and go abroad to Europe'.
(from Byram and Risager, 1998: 20–1)

Most teachers of foreign languages in Britain would echo these sentiments, I believe (see Byram and Risager, 1998 for a survey). Many would also see their responsibility for a European dimension in young people's lives as not just focused on the European Union, nor just on Europe in the much wider sense, of the 45–50 countries included in the Council of Europe for example. Teachers of French and Spanish can readily introduce global dimensions into their learners' lives by referring to francophone and hispanophone countries world-wide.

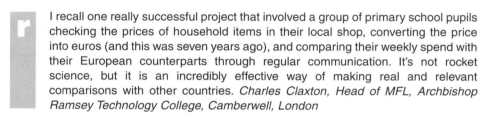

I recall one really successful project that involved a group of primary school pupils checking the prices of household items in their local shop, converting the price into euros (and this was seven years ago), and comparing their weekly spend with their European counterparts through regular communication. It's not rocket science, but it is an incredibly effective way of making real and relevant comparisons with other countries. *Charles Claxton, Head of MFL, Archbishop Ramsey Technology College, Camberwell, London*

So there is a well-established potential in language teaching to break out of the isolationism of the nation, as Dewey would see it, a potential to challenge the taken-for-granted values and pre-conceptions – including prejudiced views of other people from different countries and communities – which children acquire at an early age. Unfortunately, that potential is not always realised because of a concern for getting high grades in examinations focused on linguistic skills. This is a significant problem which cannot be pursued here (see Byram and Risager, 1998: Chapter 4), but which has to be confronted in our discussions at some point.

Yet this potential is still a limited one and what I want to propose in this article is a vision and purpose for foreign language teaching of all kinds, not just European languages, which articulates the relationship between language-and-culture learning and education for democratic citizenship.

It is a vision which is rooted both in existing classroom practices and in major political declarations. It is a vision in which practical language skills and knowledge are crucial to participation in democratic practices, but also a vision in which education about others' languages and cultures is a fundamental task for teachers. This latter task is more complex and difficult than the first because it involves values and judgements, not merely skills and knowledge.

The European perspective

There are two similar but distinctive views of language learning at the European level. In Western Europe, including Britain, it is the European Union view which dominates, expressed most cogently in a 'White Paper' from the European Commission in 1995. Here there are two functions for language learning, first to create the means of benefiting from a single market, now all the stronger because of the Euro:

> *Proficiency in several Community (i.e. EU) languages has become a precondition if citizens of the European Union are to benefit from the occupational and personal opportunities open to them in the border-free single market. This language proficiency must be backed up by the ability to adapt to working and living environments characterised by different cultures.*

... and, second, to create the means of interacting with other Europeans, in this case Europeans defined as those who belong to the EU and have voting rights for the European Parliament:

> *Languages are also the key to knowing other people. Proficiency in languages helps to build up the feeling of being European with all its cultural wealth and diversity, and of understanding between the citizens of Europe.* (European Commission, 1995: 67)

The White Paper goes on to recommend that European citizens should master three languages, their own and two of the other official languages of the EU.

The second view, that of the Council of Europe, is influenced by the much larger number of member states and by their belonging not to an economy-based organisation but to one concerned with political and cultural co-operation. A Committee of Ministers from member states defined their vision of Europe in 1999 as:

> *... a freer, more tolerant and just society based on solidarity, common values and a cultural heritage enriched by its diversity. (Council of Europe, 1999)*

This involved a view of democratic citizenship as equipping people to play an active role in their own lives and societies, preparing them to live in a multi-cultural society, strengthening social cohesion, mutual understanding and solidarity.

Recommendations for language learning to underpin this vision are encapsulated in the concept of 'plurilingualism', rather than a suggestion for a specific number of languages. Plurilingualism is defined in the *Common European Framework*, a handbook for language professionals, as:

> *... the ability to use languages for the purposes of communication and to take part in intercultural interaction, where a person, viewed as a social agent, has proficiency of varying degrees, in several languages, and experience of several cultures. This is not seen as the superposition or juxtaposition of*

> *distinct competences, but rather as the existence of a complex or even composite competence on which the user may draw.*
> (Council of Europe, 2001: 168)

For language teaching practice, this concept of plurilingualism has many implications, only some of which are yet realised. For the notion of plurilingualism suggests that learners have a complex language capacity, drawing on whatever 'bits' of language and processes of language learning they need in order to interact with people from other countries and communities (Herdina and Jessner, 2001). They do not separate their languages; they do not speak all or even any of their languages 'perfectly'; they do not rely only on linguistic skills; they combine and mix to meet the demands of the moment. Yet in language teaching, we encourage separation, purism, perfection in language learning, most obviously by curriculum and timetable arrangements but also by 'correcting' the use of French in a German lesson, or Spanish in a French lesson, when learners may in fact be drawing on their plurilingualism, being as effective as possible at that point in time. In this they resemble the millions of natural plurilinguals - in global terms the majority case - who acquire a range of languages and language varieties and use them in whatever 'mix' seems most effective.

In doing this in their limited way and despite the curriculum labels which say this is a French lesson and not a Spanish lesson, learners are unconsciously challenging the language teacher to become a teacher of languages, someone whose concern is to enable learners to develop a linguistic capacity and a potential for intercultural communication whatever the circumstances in which they find themselves. Although there are many who teach two languages, perhaps even to the same pupils, the cross-linguistic connections are not often made. Furthermore, it is an oft-lamented 'disadvantage' in motivating learners whose first language is English that English is a dominant international language. However, if language teachers see themselves as language professionals, people able to introduce young people to experience of other ways of thinking, valuing and behaving, other cultures, they would find their task easier. The aims of language teaching should include for example developing in speakers of English an ability to adapt their language to the competence levels of non-native speakers. They should also include inciting that interest in language and otherness which is central to the notion of language awareness, a concept which seems to have been lost from the national curriculum, despite the lip-service paid, because it is seen as in tension with progression towards the unattainable goal of near-native competence.

Plurilingualism combined with linguistic and cultural awareness is a much more sensible educational purpose for language teachers in English-speaking countries than the exclusive pursuit of perfection in just one or two separate languages, neither of which may be used later. For the instrumental purpose of teaching languages – languages for use, languages for business and commerce – has come to dominate the political thinking of the profession as a consequence of a more general view of 'education as our best economic policy', as Prime Minister Blair once put it. Yet even this purpose can be better served by the pursuit of plurilingualism and the flexibility it brings. From this perspective, even the European Union concept is still a traditional one, in which languages are seen as separate entities.

Whichever European perspective is taken – an EU three-language, free-market competence or a CoE plurilingual, cultural diversity competence – they share a vision of Europeans living, working, acting together in participatory democratic and multilingual social groups. The groups may be small and informal: an international colonie de vacances, or a local community of mixed ethnicities, or large and formal: an international pressure group for human rights for asylum seekers, or international trades union and employers' federations. In all of these cases single-language linguistic skills are necessary but not sufficient, and in all such encounters it is not the perfection of one language, which is perhaps not even present in a given situation, but rather the flexibility of plurilingualism and the ability to adapt one's native language to non-native environments, which is most important.

Moreover, linguistic skills need to be complemented by understanding, by what the EU White Paper calls 'a feeling of being European', by an ability to decentre and understand how others see themselves – and how they see us. Without this, exchange of information will lead to misunderstanding rather than understanding. In other words, linguistic competence needs to be complemented by intercultural competence and it is here that language teaching makes a substantial contribution to citizenship education. It is of course one of the aims of all humanistic education to help learners to see and experience other perspectives, through the imagination in the study of literature or history, through informed analysis of other countries and cultures in geography, for example, and multicultural education focused on ethnic variety in our own society is the most recent embodiment of this. Language teaching in 'pre-communicative' forms was part of this interpretation of education, but the move to 'communicative' language teaching, justified though it was in many ways, led to an abandonment of humanistic aims. These should be reclaimed and reintroduced. Language teaching is the means of re-thinking and re-experiencing the taken-for-granted world we acquire in primary and secondary socialisation because it can offer a challenge through experiential learning to the values, beliefs and behaviours which are embodied in our native language(s). A sense of citizenship which is international pre-supposes the ability to accept other perspectives, and language teaching can and should complement the teaching of English, history and geography to take young people out of their first language(s) and into another way of thinking and feeling. This is the political significance of intercultural competence.

The concept of plurilingualism suggests a completely different way of working in the MFL classroom, where explicit links are made between different languages.

- Try looking for patterns with your students, for example, in counting up to ten or in verb endings, across a number of related languages.
- Discuss this approach with your colleagues – how might it change your practice across the department?

The limitations of the European perspective

It is not surprising, that foreign languages teachers, both 'modern' and 'classical', tend to focus on the European perspective. They themselves are among the best examples of the citizens of Europe envisaged by the Council of Europe and the European Union, even if they are much more aware of Western than Eastern Europe – all the more since the unfortunate fall in interest for Russian and Slavic languages. As pointed out in the Introduction, the majority of language teachers in Britain have had a unique experience of living in another European country during their higher education and often develop a feeling of being European, as the following extract from an interview with a student returned from France suggests:

> I would say I was European rather than English (...) I would love to be French, but you can't. I can never be French because you have to be born French. I could be a European, I couldn't be French though. There's no way you can become French. You could live in France, you could speak French, but you'll never be French unless you're actually born French. (Byram and Alred 1993: 54)

So for 'Lynn' national identity is something innate whereas European identity is something which develops from experience, an experience which was fundamental to her language learning. Ten years later, Lynn was an office manager in an international legal firm in Brussels, but nonetheless thinking of re-training as a teacher. If she does become a teacher, she will be able to draw on her experience of European identity and not just on her language skills, to educate her pupils – if the education system allowed her to do so.

Currently, if Lynn were to return to Britain to teach French, she would feel a pressure to concentrate on a number of narrow national curriculum topics, using textbooks which scarcely envisage French as a language spoken outside France. She would not have the space to use her rich experience of life in multinational Brussels in her wish to educate children. Furthermore, she would not have an appropriate methodology since most language teaching methods focus exclusively on instilling acquisition of skills and cognitive knowledge of language and culture, but not the ways in which teachers should handle education in values, in moral development, in emotional response to a challenge to one's taken-for-granted world. I shall return to this problem later.

The 'European identity' of most language teachers in Britain remains nonetheless a limitation, even if we can find a methodology which allows them to use it. Language learning can and should be a challenge to the isolationism of the nation-state, but should not simply replace it by a new European isolationism, a reinforcement of the 'fortress Europe' mentality which is increasingly apparent in border controls and asylum regulations. Education for citizenship, it is often claimed, should encourage young people to see themselves locally and globally.

Teachers of European languages need to look for links to the wider world and have been encouraged to do so by some textbook writers already in the 1980s (Aplin, Miller and Starkey, 1985; Miller and Roselmann, 1988). Both Starkey and Cates have argued consistently for a link with Human Rights and Citizenship education, and made concrete proposals which have yet to be taken up and generalised (Starkey, 1999, 2000, in press; Cates, 2000).

For some teachers this will seem too ambitious. It is already difficult, they might say, to bridge the gap between Britain and the rest of Europe, as the teachers quoted earlier suggested. Our response must be both practical and persuasive in principle. On the question of principle we might turn to the work of the American Conference on the Teaching of Foreign Languages (ACTFL) which has similar and perhaps more difficult problems of overcoming isolationist thinking when arguing for language learning as part of compulsory education in American schools.

When challenged to explain why young citizens of the USA, who are very unlikely to travel beyond its frontiers, should learn foreign languages, the ACTFL reply is 'They should learn languages precisely because they will **not** travel', and this apparent paradox encapsulates the educational value of language learning even where it has no practical application. The same principle applies to young Europeans, many of whom will not travel beyond western Europe, but all of whom need to experience not just a feeling of being European in its fullest sense but also a feeling of being part of a global community.

This principle is fundamental to this book and given further explanation throughout. In my final section I want to return to the practical issues which follow from it.

FOREIGN LANGUAGE EDUCATION AS VALUES EDUCATION

> *You see, I mean I'm not just here to get As and Bs and Cs at GCSE. That's important, it's a very important part of my role in the classroom, but I think there's a much wider role, and that there's a specific wider role linked with languages (...) I often say to my classes, you know, 'Were you watching the news last night?' – at the beginning or at the end of a lesson, maybe, when we're rounding off. 'Did you think of me last night, when you were watching the news?' Because it was something that happened, you know, the problems they're having in Germany at the moment, or whatever. Because I want them to think that it's not just something they do in my classroom two or three times a week and that's it. There are people who speak that language and there are problems that those people have and they should be aware of that. (Byram and Risager, 1998: 103)*

This British teacher of German has no doubt about her responsibilities and has found a way of reconciling examination demands and the 'specific wider role linked with languages'. She also has a method, which involves breaking the taboo of speaking English in the classroom, but which also implies that equally important purposes do not require equal amounts of time. The few minutes at the beginning or end of a lesson are just as effective in citizenship education as the half hour given to linguistic matters.

What the teacher does not tell us is how she handles questions from pupils or the protests some might raise if she makes comparisons between Germany and Britain. Other teachers in our survey spoke of the need to 'break down prejudices and develop tolerance', but few if any felt they had been trained to do this. Many teachers assume that providing information and developing young people's knowledge about other countries, cultures and communities will lead to greater tolerance and break down prejudice. Yet already in his classic book of the 1950s on *The nature of prejudice*, Allport (1954) demonstrated that there is little or no evidence that more knowledge has a positive impact on prejudice.

As pointed out at the beginning of this chapter, language teaching has a well-established potential for values education. I have suggested elsewhere that this can be formulated as the objective of developing 'critical cultural awareness' in young people, the ability to juxtapose and reflect on their own ways of living, thinking and believing and those of people of a different language and culture (Byram, 1997). Increasingly, there are examples of teachers taking this seriously and developing appropriate methods for different age groups and levels of linguistic competence.

In one example, teachers of English and French in Latvia devised lessons in which learners reflected on their different ethnic identities and citizenship status at a time when Latvia was re-establishing its post-communist identity (Kalnberzina, 2001). In another, a teacher of English in Bulgaria asked pupils to compare British and Bulgarian Christmas cards. They began to gain new insights into the post-communist introduction of charity organisations with social responsibilities, a phenomenon not known and not needed in communist Bulgaria (Tupozova, 2001). These examples may appear exotic to British teachers of languages, but make explicit the direct relationships between education for citizenship and language teaching. It is perhaps not surprising that teachers in former Soviet-dominated societies are more conscious of their political role, but such examples could easily be adapted to the needs of multicultural and multilingual Britain where issues of identity and caring for the poor are no less significant than in East and Central Europe.

Mike Byram draws attention to the fact that language teachers are not usually trained to deal with comments from students that may be racist or stereotypical. They often view it as beyond their remit, or impossible to do if they are working in the target language.

- Talk to teachers in humanities departments and those who teach religious studies and PSHE and find out about the strategies they use to encourage discussion and examination of views expressed by students.

If you feel strongly enough that you want to address citizenship issues in MFL, there will be occasions where it will be important to give the students the chance to express their views in English. Try it and see how your students respond.

The potential for language teaching to contribute to citizenship is evident and realisable. On the other hand, language teaching could benefit significantly from the methodology of education for citizenship. It can find help in dealing with inevitable conflicts of values, in developing moral and affective learning, in clarifying the position of the teacher. For there are doubtless many teachers who share Lynn's enthusiasm about the language and people who have significant experiences in their lives, but enthusiasm is not enough. It needs to be tempered by responsibility and a conscious acknowledgement of the 'specific wider role' of language teaching. This is one of the most important issues facing the integration of language teaching and education for citizenship in the coming years.

Bibliography

Allport, (1954), *The nature of prejudice.* Cambridge, Mass.: Addison-Wesley.

Aplin, R., Miller, A. and Starkey, H. (1985), *Orientations.* Hodder and Stoughton.

Byram, M. (1997) *Teaching and assessing intercultural communicative competence.* Multilingual Matters.

Byram, M. and Alred, G. (1993) *Paid to be English: a book for English assistants and their advisers in France.* Durham University: School of Education.

Byram, M. and Risager, K. (1998) *Language teachers, politics and cultures.* Multilingual Matters.

Cates, K. (2000) 'Global education'. In M. Byram (ed) *Routledge Encyclopedia of language teaching and learning.* Routledge.

Council of Europe (1999) Declaration and programme of action 99 (76) of the Committee of Ministers on *Education for democratic citizenship based on the rights and responsibilities of citizens.* Strasbourg: Council of Europe.

Council of Europe (2001) *Common European Framework of reference for languages: learning, teaching, assessment.* Cambridge University Press.

European Commission (1995) *White Paper on Education and Training. Teaching and learning – towards the learning society.* Luxembourg: Office for Official Publications of the European Union.

Herdina, P. and Jessner, U. (2001) *A dynamic model of multilingualism.* Multilingual Matters.

Kalnberzina, V. (2001) 'Understanding social identity: a module for advanced learners'. In

Byram, M. and Tost Planet, M, (eds) *Social identity and the european dimension. Intercultural competence through foreign language learning.* Graz: Council of Europe. (also available on-line at the European Centre for Modern Languages, Graz, Austria).

Miller, A. and Roselmann, E. (1988) *Arc-en-ciel.* Mary Glasgow Publications.

Starkey, H. (1999) 'Foreign language teaching to adults: implicit and explicit political education'. In: *Oxford Review of Education:* Vol. 25, Nos 1 & 2, pp155–170.

Starkey, H. (2000) 'Human Rights'. In: Byram, M. (ed) *Encyclopedia of language teaching and learning.* Routledge.

Starkey, H. (in press) *Intercultural competence and education for democratic citizenship: implications for language teaching methodology.* Strasbourg: Council of Europe.

Tupozova, K. (2001) 'British and Bulgarian Christmas cards. A research project for students'. In Byram, M., Nichols, A. and Stevens, D. (eds) *Developing intercultural competence in practice.* Multilingual Matters.

Chapter 2

Language teaching for cosmopolitan citizenship

Hugh Starkey and Audrey Osler

The authors of this chapter look at aspects of language teaching which are already familiar to us, cultural awareness and communicative language teaching, and show how these are central to teaching about citizenship. They focus particularly on human rights issues and anti-racism and suggest ways in which language teachers can contribute to citizenship education through both the content of lessons and the way in which they are organised and managed.

Introduction: cosmopolitan citizenship

Language learning can be an intercultural experience. It has the potential to help learners to develop their identities as cosmopolitan citizens in a global context. Cosmopolitan citizens recognise that their human rights confirm their common humanity with all the people of the world. In the defence of human rights and the promotion of democracy they are in solidarity with all those aspiring to these aims. They hold to the principles enshrined in the Charter of the United Nations (Held, 1995).

The National Curriculum for England makes the claim that:

> *Through the study of foreign languages, pupils understand and appreciate different countries, cultures, people and communities – and as they do so, begin to* **think of themselves as citizens of the world** *as well as of the United Kingdom. (Department for Education and Employment, 1999: 14)* (our emphasis)

Language courses can be sites for developing democracy and fuller understandings of citizenship. Through the content of their language courses, learners can acquire knowledge of human rights. Since human rights are based on the premise that all human beings have equal rights and equal entitlement to respect and dignity, they may be considered to be universal principles. As the report of the Nuffield Languages Inquiry recommends:

> *Direct links should be established in school education between language learning and education for citizenship, so as to foster* **notions of equality and acceptance of diversity** *in children's minds at the earliest possible age.* (The Nuffield Languages Inquiry, 2000: 32) (our emphasis)

This recommendation, while not mentioning human rights, refers specifically to the key human rights principles of equality and diversity. The Scottish report on languages, *Citizens of a multilingual world,* also spells out this potential contribution to citizenship education:

> *We consider that education in languages at school has an essential role to play in preparing all students for citizenship of the wider society. If it helps them become sensitive to the languages and cultures of others and develops in them sufficient confidence and competence to be able to use their languages, however modestly, in their interactions with other citizens, then we believe they are more likely to understand others and to be respected by them. In this way* **the wider society becomes more open, democratic and inclusive.** (Ministerial Action Group on Languages, 2000: 2) (our emphasis)

Negativity and its consequences

The potential of language teaching is one thing. The reality, in Britain, is often very different. Research from Scotland notes that by age thirteen:

> *... a significant minority had 'switched off'. ... Those students ... who had 'switched off' were not only unable to see any real point in languages but* **their self-image and self-confidence had been negatively affected**, *to the extent that for them learning and using another language was stressful and anxiety inducing.* (Ministerial Action Group on Languages, 2000: 8) (our emphasis)

Indeed, the report quotes an earlier study of 100 Scottish schools that identified a 'climate of negativity' that was affecting languages at school. The finding is confirmed, for England, by the Nuffield Languages Inquiry.

> *Too many pupils – including those achieving high grades – emerge from secondary education with limited practical competence, low levels of confidence and* **negative attitudes towards language learning.** (The Nuffield Languages Inquiry, 2000: 45) (our emphasis)

In other words, the reality of much language teaching and learning is that it may in fact produce citizens with a negative approach to languages. It is even possible that the experience of language learning actually reinforces xenophobia.

If language learning is really to be a significant contribution to citizenship education, teachers and course writers need to engage with and address negative attitudes to languages and to the people and cultures associated with particular languages. Fortunately, research suggests that a majority of language teachers feel professionally committed to combating stereotypes and helping to overcome prejudice (Byram and Risager, 1999). This chapter suggests what this may mean in practice.

Citizenship, democracy and antiracism

Language teaching and learning for citizenship is about enabling democratic participation, overcoming barriers and crossing boundaries. This requires both a cross-cultural approach, focusing on diversity between societies, and a simultaneous intercultural approach which acknowledges the diversity within societies (Kramsch, 1998). When they are infused with an understanding of and commitment to human rights, both approaches may help to break down stereotypes.

However, for the development of a pluralist democratic society, foreign language skills and intercultural understanding are not in themselves sufficient. One of the major barriers to democratic participation in Europe today is that of racism and xenophobia which contribute to structural inequality and exclusion. Thus any course, including a foreign language course, that seeks to develop learning for democracy needs to address racism as a barrier to full participation, to consider the position of minority and majority populations within society, and allow students to explore issues of identity (Osler and Starkey, 1996).

Citizenship describes the relationship of individuals to communities and to governments where human rights are agreed standards. Racism denies the principle of equal human dignity without which there can be no concept of human rights. Human rights and antiracism are therefore inseparable. (Osler and Starkey, 1996, 2000; Starkey, 2000; Starkey and Osler, 2001). It follows that a commitment to antiracism is not a negative position but a positive contribution to promoting democracy and removing barriers to citizenship (Bonnett, 2000; Lloyd, 1998).

Recent attempts to define racism emphasise the pervasive influence of stereotypes.

> *Racism, in short, involves (a) stereotypes about difference and inferiority, and (b) the use of power to exclude, discriminate or subjugate.* (Parekh, 2000: 63)

Antiracism, then, involves challenging stereotypes and examining ways in which groups are discriminated against, excluded or subjugated. Teachers can help learners recognise unfairly discriminating practices and uses of power in relation to cultures and groups. Students may then be helped to recognise that:

> *Racism is a subtle and complex phenomenon. It may be based on colour and physical features or on culture, nationality and way of life; it may affirm equality of human worth but implicitly deny this by insisting on the absolute superiority of a particular culture; it may admit equality up to a point, but impose a glass ceiling higher up.* (Parekh, 2000: ix)

In one community languages project, students prepared questionnaires and interviewed people who had experienced education in Bangladesh. These included parents, family members, people from the community (shopkeepers, librarians, religious leaders) or their teacher. In carrying out this kind of research, they were forced to evaluate issues from different viewpoints and to assess the supporting evidence. This involved taking account of bias, questioning assumptions, formulating hypotheses. It is a process which aspires to the creation of new knowledge and generates a sense of ownership among students.
Manju Chaudhuri

Representations of cultures

When teachers assert their commitment to overcoming prejudice, they tend to see their role as conveying knowledge about a target culture (Byram and Risager, 1999). The purpose of studying other cultures is to encourage reflective learners. Where cultures are presented in their plurality and their complexity, students are helped to de-centre and relativise their relationship with their own culture of origin. In other words, they reconsider their attitudes to what was previously considered foreign. This is one strategy for reducing xenophobia and overcoming prevalent stereotypes. Stereotyping involves labelling groups of people, usually in a negative way, according to preconceived ideas. It may be racist and is certainly undemocratic. It may be challenged in language learning, or reinforced.

Through their study of authentic materials and specially created language courses, learners have opportunities to explore and discuss aspects of target cultures other than those with which they are already familiar and make comparisons.

> *It has long been a commonplace among language teachers that their pedagogical aims include the encouragement in their learners of an interest in an opening towards a culture, people and country where the language in question is spoken.* (Byram, 1993)

However, teachers may need to provide their own materials or select them carefully from available published courses since much course material fails to give adequate coverage to cultural content. Course writers may prioritise grammar and linguistic functions over the social or the political.

A study of course materials available in Britain for teaching French as a foreign language reported that a number of courses are largely devoid of cultural references.

> *Either in its format (for instance, its style of illustration, presentation of topics) or in its linguistic content (absence of specific societal markers within the language items), the material manages to retain a neutrality in cultural matters. In a few instances, it would be reasonable to say that some material focuses on a narrow view of British culture rather than encounter any French cultural aspects whatsoever*
> (Aplin, 2000: 8).

Such courses, which fail entirely to acknowledge that there is a cultural dimension to language teaching, also miss an opportunity to engage with and challenge language learners. They do nothing to combat stereotypes.

Even where courses include an explicit cultural dimension, basic stereotypes may remain and indeed be reinforced by the materials. Another study of learning materials found that:

> *Reductionism is a problem inherent in all teaching material and it is all the more inevitable where the number of words available to cover a topic is sometimes limited to a few lines, particularly in specially written material. In such a context it is difficult to convey the diversity of cultural practices*
> (Fleig-Hamm, 1998) (our translation).

Thus there are some textbooks that deny that studying a language necessarily means studying cultures and there are others that depict cultures so summarily that they fail to challenge learners. A culture presented as uniform and without complexity is likely to be stereotyped to the point of absurdity.

Choosing topics for cosmopolitan citizenship

Citizenship is about the public sphere and about understanding of and engagement with policies. One of the reasons for language learning being associated with negativity may well be that the topics of study for languages are mainly associated with the private sphere. As such they fail to engage with political issues and lack intellectual stimulation for lively young minds. A logical response to negativity and low motivation may well be consciously to introduce the public sphere and give a citizenship dimension to the topics.

Many courses use scenarios that involve young people visiting a country associated with the target language and attempt to give the learner a role as actor in an intercultural setting. However, since the purpose imagined for the visit is often tourism, the language learner is frequently represented in course material not as citizen but as child within the family, pupil within the school and consumer within society. There is rarely a suggestion that students will take with them any curiosity or any social, historical, economic or political awareness.

In fact, although the programmes of study for Key Stages 3 and 4 have been freed of specific content, the influence of examinations often results in learners remaining confined to the private sphere for the five years of their secondary schooling. The speaking test in GCSE French, for instance is based on:

- home life
- school life
- self, family and friends
- free time
- your local area
- careers, work, work experience
- holidays (Oxford Cambridge and RSA Examinations, 2000b)

The list of topics provides no encouragement to learners to look outside their own personal sphere. Even interest in the target culture can only be evoked in the context of holidays. For one teacher, this limited conception of language learning directly contributes to lack of engagement by the learners.

> *Perhaps the biggest problem (and the main cause of boredom) is that those topics are visited and revisited year after year adding on a little more vocabulary each time.* (Callaghan, 1998: 6)

This challenge to language teachers is also highlighted in the report *Citizens of a Multilingual World*:

> *The languages curriculum is perceived by students as **intrinsically** motivating to begin with through association with interesting and pleasurable activities at primary school, but **that intrinsic motivation declines** at secondary school when students begin to perceive in it a lack of intellectual stimulation and a lack of deep engagement with their real and emerging adolescent interests.* (Ministerial Action Group on Languages, 2000: 9) (original emphasis)

Given this lack of engagement with the public sphere and the interests of adolescent learners, it is perhaps not surprising that language teachers have recently tended to see themselves as developing skills rather than cultural knowledge (Byram and Risager, 1999).

Opportunities for teaching citizenship through languages

It is possible to teach citizenship in the target language and still cover the restricted GCSE list of topics, as some course books have demonstrated (Aplin, Miller and Starkey, 1985; Miller, Roselman, and Bougard, 1990). Questions of health, lifestyle, and life projects taught in the language studied can include both a political and a comparative cultural dimension. For example, policies on smoking in public places may well have a direct relevance to learners' lives and be a topic of lively discussion in the target language.

Themes treated as personal can also be challenged by bringing in a public or policy dimension and using an intercultural and critical perspective. Learners compare the theme in a familiar situation with examples from an unfamiliar context. For instance the theme of **sport** can be examined from many perspectives, including:

- Gender – are there sports that are, in the familiar context or in the unfamiliar context, predominantly played by men or by women? Are things changing? Which sports and teams attract the most media attention and funding, men's or women's?

- Religion – are there religious objections to playing sport, or days when some people choose not to do sport because of religious observance?

- Racism – is this found in spectator sports? Are the players of foreign teams, or foreign players in local teams always treated with respect? Are there incidents of racist chants or insults?

Advanced learners

Advanced level syllabuses provide many opportunities to engage with issues relevant to citizenship. One, for example, includes the study of far right political parties in France and Germany and terrorist organisations in Spain (Oxford Cambridge and RSA Examinations, 2000a). In a democratic society it must be assumed that this has been chosen in order to demonstrate the unacceptability of the discourses and actions of such movements. An understanding of human rights as the basis for democracy is essential background for such study. This is particularly important when preparing an essay topic such as one proposed in the specimen material, namely: 'Explain the success of the National Front among some sections of the French population' (Oxford Cambridge and RSA Examinations, 2000a). Teachers will need to make explicit to students that this is not an invitation to rehearse or justify the racist policies of the National Front, but an opportunity to develop an understanding of human rights and the racist nature of some FN policies. A title such as 'Explain why some of the policies of the National Front are in contradiction with the basic principles of the French Republic' might be more effective in ensuring this is the outcome of the essay task.

At advanced level, one important contribution to antiracism is the inclusion of vocabulary that helps learners talk about cultural diversity. This can include terms such as: human rights; equality; dignity; gender; bias; prejudice; stereotype; racism; ethnic minority; and the names of ethnic groups, including white groups.

Democratic discussion

The pedagogy associated with language learning provides a further contribution of languages to citizenship. In many respects communicative methodology is in itself democratic. The skills developed in language classes are thus directly transferable to citizenship education.

> *The communicative language classroom implies that priority is given to speech acts. The role of the teacher is to guide pupils in their use of the new communicative tool, the second language. Teachers will be concerned not just with linguistic achievements, but with communicative competence as an end in itself. Skills (savoir faire) such as ability to listen, to reformulate the words of another the better to understand them, put a different point of view, produce a valid argument, conceding are all life skills (savoir être) with applicability elsewhere in school and in the outside world ... The language class is a site where education for dialogue is especially developed. (Tardieu, 1999: 24) (our translation).*

In the communicative language classroom learners are often required to speak and discuss in pairs and groups, having the freedom to express their own opinions and develop ideas and new ways of thinking. This contribution to the overall project of democratic citizenship can also be recognised and developed. Since discussion and debate require working with others, taking part in public discourse and working to resolve conflicts, language teaching can contribute substantially to capacities for action and social competencies.

Whether the context is pair work, group work or discussions involving the whole class, teachers taking a human rights position insist on ground rules. This can help to ensure that expressions of opinion and conflicts of views are productive and not destructive. The guidance for teachers produced for the Key Stage 3 Scheme of Work for Citizenship gives the following advice:

> *It is essential that pupils develop their own ground rules rather than be presented with ones produced elsewhere ...*

> *Pupils should be regularly reminded of the ground rules and their importance when handling sensitive issues appropriately during whole-class and group discussion.*

The following ground rules are examples of ones established by pupils:

- *Listen to each other.*
- *Make sure everyone has a chance to speak.*
- *Don't use 'put downs' or make fun of what others say or do.*
- *Be helpful and constructive when challenging another's viewpoint.*
- *Offer help and support when it is needed.*
- *You have a right to 'pass' if you do not want to speak on an issue.*
- *Show appreciation when someone explains or does something well, or is helpful in some way to you.* (Qualifications and Curriculum Authority, 2001, p38)

Although this guidance suggests that the ground rules should come from the pupils, teachers can feed in suggestions and might consider the following additional points:

- Where a discussion is chaired, the authority of the chair is respected.

- Even heated debates must be conducted in polite language.

- Discriminatory remarks, particularly racist, sexist and homophobic discourse and expressions are totally unacceptable at any time.

- Participants show respect when commenting on and describing people portrayed in visuals or texts.

- All involved have the responsibility to challenge stereotypes.

- A respectful tone is required at all times.

It goes without saying that teachers are party to these agreements and will not use sarcasm, irony and disparaging judgements.

- To what extent do you feel your language classroom is a democratic one?

- List as many teacher-pupil and pupil-pupil interactions as you can in a typical language lesson.

- Ask yourself: who initiates interactions, who asks questions and who answers them, how much pupil talking time do you think there is in each lesson, to what extent are pupils involved in planning and managing of lessons etc?

- Why not discuss this at a staff meeting and find out about each others' classrooms. What can you learn from each other?

- You might like to suggest that you monitor each other's classroom to gain a clearer sense of how democratic they are (see page 11 for further discussion of this point).

Conclusion

The pedagogy of communicative language teaching is based on the democratic principles of freedom of expression and equal opportunities for participation. There is considerable freedom for teachers to adapt topics to include the public sphere and help learners understand human rights and cosmopolitan citizenship in a multicultural and multilingual world. In order to ensure that the study of other cultures is an experience that opens rather than closes minds, language teaching needs to address racism and xenophobia directly. By engaging with serious topics including the public sphere teachers may provide motivation and raise standards as well as helping to create cosmopolitan citizens able to operate effectively in a range of cultural contexts.

Bibliography

Aplin, R. (2000). Images of France: cultural awareness in French language teaching materials. *Francophonie* (22), 6–10.

Aplin, R., Miller, A. and Starkey, H. (1985) *Orientations*. Hodder & Stoughton.

Bonnett, A. (2000) *Anti-racism*. Routledge.

Byram, M. (1993) 'Introduction: culture and language learning in higher education'. *Language, culture and curriculum, 6*, 1–3.

Byram, M. and Risager, K. (1999) *Language teachers, politics and cultures*. Multilingual Matters.

Callaghan, M. (1998). 'An investigation into the causes of boys' underachievement in French'. *Language Learning Journal, 17*, 2–7.

Department for Education and Employment (1999) *The National Curriculum for England*.

Fleig-Hamm, C. (1998) 'La francophonie dans les manuels de français langue seconde: apports et limites'. *La revue canadienne des langues vivantes, 54* (4).

Held, D. (1995) 'Democracy and the new international order'. In: Archibugi, D. and Held, D. (eds) *Cosmopolitan democracy* (pp96–120). Polity Press.

Kramsch, C. (1998) *Language and culture*. Oxford University Press.

Lloyd, C. (1998) *Discourses of antiracism in France*. Ashgate.

Miller, A., Roselman, L., and Bougard, M. (1990) *Arc-en-ciel*. Mary Glasgow Publications.

Ministerial Action Group on Languages (2000) *Citizens of a multilingual world*. Scottish Executive Education Department.

Osler, A. and Starkey, H. (1996) *Teacher education and human rights*. Fulton.

Osler, A. and Starkey, H. (2000) 'Intercultural education and foreign language learning: issues of racism, identity and modernity'. In: *Race, ethnicity and education, 3* (2), 231–245.

Oxford Cambridge and RSA Examinations (2000a) *OCR Advanced Subsidiary and Advanced GCE in French German and Spanish*. OCR.

Oxford Cambridge and RSA Examinations (2000b) *OCR GCSEs in French, German, Spanish and Gujerati*. OCR.

Qualifications and Curriculum Authority (2001) *Citizenship. A scheme of work for Key Stage 3. Teacher's guide*.

Starkey, H. (2000) 'Human rights'. In: Byram, M. (ed) *Encyclopedia of language teaching and learning*. Routledge.

Starkey, H. and Osler, A. (2001) 'Language learning and antiracism: some pedagogical challenges'. *The Curriculum Journal, 12* (3), 313–329.

Tardieu, C. (1999) *Le professeur citoyen*. Bourg-la-Reine: Editions M.T.

The Nuffield Languages Inquiry (2000) *Languages: the next generation*. The Nuffield Foundation.

Chapter 3

Spanish Voices: today's children, tomorrow's world

An Internet project linking young Spanish-speakers around the world

Margaret Burr

In this chapter, Margaret Burr gives us a flavour and practical examples of an e-mail exchange project she set up with language learners in four different Spanish-speaking communities across the world. The words of the pupils taking part as well as of those adults who encouraged and supported them give teachers everywhere an inspirational model to follow.

Introduction and context

This chapter will introduce the Internet linking project, *Spanish Voices,* which brought together young people from communities in the Spanish-speaking world using the framework of the *UN Convention on the Rights of the Child.* The four communities were Guatemala, Spain, Western Saharan refugees in Algeria and students studying Spanish in Tower Hamlets.

Rationale for less familiar issues in MFL

The *Spanish Voices* project fitted closely with National Curriculum requirements to communicate in the target language and achieve cultural awareness. Modern language inspector Chris Brocklesby saw *Spanish Voices* as being able to '*deliver parts of the modern languages curriculum to areas that textbooks can't reach'.* At first the *UN Convention on the Rights of the Child* might appear a rather complex framework, however, it is ideal for providing issues for discussion and debate, which young people can relate to and have experienced.

In the *Spanish Voices* project, those rights that related particularly to Part II: Areas of Experience of the MFL National Curriculum were reinterpreted so that 'home life and school' became the Right to a Home, the Right to Education and so on, leading to five sections:

- identity (myself and my country);
- home and environment;
- education and work;
- food and leisure;
- religion, tradition and celebrations.

This slight change of focus facilitated the use of language to present situations in new and exciting ways as well as introducing vocabulary of less familiar issues raised in discussions on global citizenship such as fair trade, debt, tourism, war and refugees. This can be seen in some of the questions exchanged. *'What sort of home do you live in?* is the kind of question children often ask each other in language lessons. The answer is usually fairly predictable – a house, a flat, a bungalow. But from the Western Sahara and Guatemala the replies received, in Spanish, were *'in a tent'* and *'in a shack by the rubbish dump'*.

The curriculum emphasised cultural awareness, stating that pupils should be given opportunities to: work with authentic materials; come into contact with native speakers; consider their own cultures and compare it with the culture of the countries and communities where the target languages is spoken; identify with the experiences and perspectives of people in these countries; and recognise cultural attitudes as expressed in the language. An Internet project such as *Spanish Voices* with contributions from a range of communities clearly provided the opportunities for all of the above; however, a link with any other country can also fulfil those requirements. It is important to support any e-mail-based project with the exchange of other materials. These can be young people's own drawings or photographs, for example, but also local information guides, maps, articles and other authentic materials. E-mail may appear a cold, impersonal medium, but this need not be the case and information that is exchanged clearly enables people to identify with others' experiences. As Mazharia said: *'It's fun sending messages and learning about their feelings and the way they live.'*

The methodology of language teaching reflects the collaborative and democractic processes used by development education practitioners. Students can be encouraged to communicate in pairs and groups, to take part in imaginative and creative activities such as role-plays, games and improvised drama, and to discuss their ideas and experiences.

Value in exchanges and e-mail links

The purpose of any link is to enrich the learning of pupils and with e-mail there are benefits for both teacher and pupil. Spanish teacher Josune Iriondo liked the idea of *'learning with my students. I'll know very little more than they do about the lives of the children we're communicating with'*. Direct contact enables students to take responsibility for their own learning, providing them with the opportunity to have their own questions answered and their views and opinions valued. There is a vitality to e-mails which motivates and stimulates students through enabling them to 'meet' other young people. Providing young people with the opportunity to set the agenda through leading the communications is more likely to sustain their interest and enthusiasm. Charmaine commented: *'The project takes more time than if we had a textbook, but it is exciting being able to ask questions directly of the other children.'*

Such communications can also inform debate, heighten awareness of issues encountered by others and provide the opportunity to develop empathy and challenge stereotypes and prejudices. Such links also empower young people, facilitating opportunities for collaboration on real issues and giving them a voice. The *Spanish Voices* project for example led to participation by young people in a Radio 4 programme, an exhibition on the Internet, the BBC Spanish language series based on the project, *Voces Españolas*, and several articles in papers and magazines. As Davinder commented: *'Some of the questions are quite hard to answer but some are easy to translate. I have learnt a lot more words by doing this project'*, and Shuly said quite simply: *'It is improving my Spanish.'*

As most people are aware, e-mail tends to encourage short messages, giving learners confidence and encouraging speedy communications. Similarly, shared project work in groups or classes in each community feels less pressured for teachers and students. Linking individual students, as pen pals, is possible, but needs more attention. Without care some students may feel inadequate, particularly those who have difficulty making friends. Other complications are possible, not least managing and maintaining these links over time.

Getting started

The project developed a strategy that has been taken up by other linking projects. The first step is to establish communications with your partners. The next stage is the 10/10/10 strategy: a class exercise as a starting point to introduce schools and communities to each other. Initially, students are only told the name of the country or community they will be linking with and the language spoken. In groups, they are asked to prepare:

- 10 questions for their partners: the questions have to be general with one set of questions for all partners. The students have to decide as a class which ten questions to send.

- 10 points of information about themselves: students decide, in the same way, on ten points of information about themselves. This stage must be completed before any replies have been received to ensure that their partners do not influence the information the class selects.

- 10 rights which they feel that every child should have: again students prepare lists of ten rights in their groups and as a class develop one final list to send to partners.

Any additional questions or information not included can be sent at a later stage. The question from the Saharawi 'What is your daily programme?' initially elicited the comment 'Eastenders, Señorita!' Other questions which arose later were more specific, with the Guatemalans asking the Western Saharans *'?Hay millones de estrellas en el cielo?' Are there millions of stars in the sky?* and another, more poignant one: 'If you are invaded, where will you go?'

Successes: examples of work – teacher and student perspective

As a means of sharing information the students produced four newsletters a year, each community taking responsibility for one issue, and a supplement was produced for teachers and partners of the project. Work written by pupils in a language other than their first has been left as sent by their teacher. In some cases pupils' words have been corrected. The following extracts help to give a flavour of the project from a number of different perspectives.

My ideal city

My ideal city would be very big.
Everything there would be made of chocolate and cream.
I would be able to buy everything and savour it all.
I would be able to fly and fly wherever I wanted to.
I would see many countries and I would discover many treasures.
I would paint the world full of peace and happiness.
I would play and sing with my friends.
I would bathe in the clouds and warm myself in the sun.
I would never sleep because I would always want to have fun.
There would be many flowers and butterflies even though it wasn't spring.
It would only be possible to hear silence and everything would shine.
That would be my ideal city and I would never forget it.
My ideal city would be like that and I would never ever forget it.

Loli Lorca Jiménez

Eastenders!

Este en el East End de Londres. Tower Hamlets es parte del East End de Londres. Vivimos aqui. En el East End muchos mercadillos para ir de compras como el de Whitechapel y el de Upton Park.

Hay muchos centros de recreo en el East End en donde los niños se lo puden pasar muy bien. Hay también muchos centros commerciales muy grandes como Tesco, Sainsbury, Iceland y muchos más.

Hay una serie muy famosa en la televisión que se llama 'Eastenders' y es sobre la vida de verdad en el 'Eastenders'.

Home

Most of the families in the camps are headed by women and we all live in our own tents. The number of people in a family varies from 5 to 10. Every tent has an entrance and openings for air and light. At night we all sleep together on the floor in our beds made out of blankets. The tent is the main living space but we have a kitchen and living room outside. It is a sign of hospitality and respect to serve tea whenever visitors come to our tent. Tea drinking is an important social event in our community.

Dear colleague,

I would like to state that this project is very important for us, the people of Western Sahara, and very particularly, it is important for the children of this country.

The reasons for this are several, but I will mention here only few of them: it will develop the curriculum within the schools and it will give the children in the refugee camps a wider and better understanding of the outside world. More importantly, I think, projects like this one, will give the Saharawi children a sense of support from young people in other countries and this makes them feel less isolated and reassure them that they are not being forgotten.

The project also will allow children from diverse backgrounds and experience to enhance the understanding of their respective local environment as well as enable them to learn from each other.

I do believe that this kind of projects are very beneficial for children, because they contribute to make understand each other better and this, in itself, is a great benefit for the whole humanity, since the children of today are the leaders of tomorrow.

Mohamed BEISSAT

Out of the dump Children's Photography Project of Guatemala Guatemala City February 1997

The Guatemalan Children's Photography Project '*Out of the dump*' is certain proof that the project *Spanish Voices: today's children, tomorrow's world* is having a long-term positive impact on all the participants involved, creating an educational and ultimately unifying dialogue.

The children who live on Guatemala City's municipal trash heap are not verbally articulate and so they used photography to communicate the impression of their world visually. For the children of Guatemala this project has unlimited benefits. It provides an infrastructure for introducing the concept of the rights of the child. In schools so poor that the teacher dictates all day as there are no books, imagine the stimulation of working on a project where you, the child, carry out research work, use your imagination and creativity, and share your ideas with other children around the world, learning that there is another world.

The partner communities benefit in many of the same areas: exchange of experiences with children of other cultures, learning new skills, the empowerment that comes with the child knowing he/she is part of an international project and communicating with other children that speak and write in Spanish.

It gives young people in Great Britain the opportunity to see that children who come from less fortunate circumstances are still able to communicate successfully and creatively and in some cases to overcome their difficulties. Achievements are attained by perseverance and being true to what you know. They are able to perceive first hand by communication with their peers in the partner communities how the rights of the child differ in each region. Hopefully what they are learning is that we all share common bonds and we are all the same people.

Spanish Voices is helping to get children of the North and South to communicate to each other on the global concept of basic children's rights and provide them with a means for learning how to communicate ideas. One hopes, through understanding and communication, the children will learn that differences and solutions can be resolved in peaceful, enlightened exchanges in the growing conflicts of our global community.

Nancy McGirr
Out of the dump Project co-ordinator

Problems, pitfalls

One of the key issues which affects the success of any project is communication in the widest sense. It is important to establish systems that enable partners to discuss potential difficulties and to be aware that perceptions may be very different. Other important considerations are clarifying and agreeing roles and responsibilities, and expectations of all involved. In establishing partnerships, there is a need to be clear about the benefits to all participants, since these may often not be the same, and to constantly review and reassess progress.

Links with other countries, particularly outside Europe, have additional difficulties, with the school year and holidays often being at different times, with different ways of working, different methodologies, lack of access to resources – all of which can affect the dynamic of the link. Decisions have also to be taken as to whether the link will be part of the curriculum and take place within lessons or as an out-of-school activity or both. It is vital to establish a system for communicating in both languages being used, to enable students in both communities to exchange information at their own intellectual level, as well as in their 'learner' language level.

There will inevitably be technical difficulties with both hardware and software at times and possibly with access to computers and the Internet. It is important to keep in touch with your partners and to keep them up to date with any developments that might affect the project.

Conclusion

Although the *Spanish Voices* project linked several communities, the lessons learned and outlined above apply to any link, particularly between communities speaking different languages. The framework of the *UN Convention of the Rights of the Child* is still applicable despite changes in the Modern Foreign Languages curriculum and provides many opportunities for joint project work. Working together on a common task or activity, such as can be seen in the *Imaginary City* and development of the game *Locococo*, bring such links to life and encourages creativity across a range of personal and social skills.

Bibliography

Voces Españolas (1998) BBC video pack including teacher booklet. BBC Worldwide

UN Convention on Human Rights, *Rights of the child* (plain English version) English version available from UNICEF and Spanish translation available from Humanities Education Centre

Brocklesby – Chris Brocklesby, MFL Inspector, Tower Hamlets

McDonald, F. (1998) *Child workers in Guatemala: an investigation*. In: DEA Journal Vol 4, No 2

McDonald, F. (2000) *Locococo: the Spanish Voices game*: Humanities Education Centre (available in English and Spanish).

Locococo website: www.locococo.org

Spanish Voices: today's children, tomorrow's world – Western Saharan children talk about their lives (1998). Minority Rights Group.
(leaflets available in English and Spanish from Minority Rights Group)

Chapter 4

International citizenship education: changing priorities, exchanging teachers

Ian Davies, Peter Cunningham, Mark Evans,
Gunilla Fredriksson, Graham Pike, Hanns-Fred
Rathenow, Alan Sears, Felicitas Tesch

This chapter looks at the broad political context surrounding the current interest in citizenship education and encourages us to think clearly about our own understanding of terms such as diversity, pluralism and participation. By involving student teachers in citizenship issues during their training, as the authors here have done, we can begin to build firm foundations for citizenship teaching in our schools.

Introduction

The development of citizenship education provides a key opportunity for language teachers and learners. Doyé (1996) appropriately has suggested:

> If language is considered as a system of signs, and signs are characterised by the fact that they are units of form and meaning, it is impossible to learn a language by simply acquiring the form without the content. And as the content of a language is always culture-bound, any reasonable foreign language teaching cannot but include the study of a culture from which the language stems.

In this chapter we focus on issues arising from citizenship education that require a study of culture and society. We draw attention to the current high level of interest in citizenship education and try to explain how that has come about. Some of the reasons for the increased attention given to citizenship education are not entirely positive, but we believe that by drawing attention to these issues the chances of implementing successful and professionally based work will be heightened. In short, if we know the pitfalls, we may be able to develop strategies to avoid the negative and embrace the positive. With this aim in mind, we outline towards the end of the chapter a current exchange project involving student teachers and practising teachers in three Canadian provinces and three European countries. The project is both challenging and rewarding in its exploration of ways to provide and promote citizenship education.

A current high level of interest in citizenship education

Citizenship is now one of the key concepts that we use to interpret contemporary society and our place within it. In England Professor (now Sir Bernard) Crick chaired a committee that recommended that citizenship education should be characterised in terms of social and moral responsibility, community involvement and political literacy. That led to changes to the National Curriculum with an insistence that pupils develop knowledge and understanding relevant to citizenship, skills of enquiry and skills of participation and responsible action. But the citizenship phenomenon is not restricted to England. Other parts of the United Kingdom have had for some time a proper professional concern with thinking about and preparing young people to act effectively. There have been a variety of useful initiatives over a long period of time in Scotland (e.g. *Modern Studies* and, more recently, statements from the Scottish Executive, see Arthur and Wright, 2001) and Northern Ireland (e.g. education for mutual understanding as well as more recent initiatives that are more sharply focused on citizenship). Across Europe individual states have taken action to educate about citizenship. There have also been many transnational projects led by a variety of organisations, the most significant of which has been the Council of Europe. There is also a considerable amount of interest in European citizenship itself which has had legal status since the signing of the Maastricht Treaty (see Davies, 1998). Globally there is massive interest in citizenship education which is probably illustrated most simply by reference to the recent IEA Civic Education Project (Torney-Purta, Schwille and Amadeo, 1999) which includes work from almost 30 countries in the northern and southern hemispheres. Other work on a smaller scale (e.g. Fouts, in press; Cogan and Derricott, 1998) shows the strong level of international attention being devoted to citizenship education.

This high level of interest is of recent origin (Davies, 1999). Although it would be inappropriate to be overly negative, it seems reasonable to assert that before the 1970s very little, if anything, was done explicitly for citizenship education. While schools are intensely political institutions with clear ideological preferences, there has been very little evidence of explicit and effective citizenship education in the classroom. Those who in the past went to look for political education programmes (e.g. Stradling and Noctor, 1981; Fogelman, 1991) tended not to find them. Crick and Heater (1977) explained the reasons for this neglect: a lack of tradition in this field, few teachers professionally committed to it, a belief that politics is solely an adult domain and a fear of indoctrination.

What then can explain this dramatic shift to a high level of interest? Four factors may be significant. These factors will be stated negatively for the purpose of emphasising the caution that teachers will need to employ when promoting citizenship education:

- There is a perceived need to differentiate clearly between those who have a legal right to stay in a country and those who do not. The connection in England between the Home Office (responsible for law and order and immigration) and citizenship education needs to be emphasised. John Patten was a junior minister in the Home Office interested in citizenship prior to becoming the Secretary of State for Education who made an attempt to implement this form of education as a cross-curricular theme. David Blunkett as Secretary of State for Education was responsible for the introduction of citizenship education into the National Curriculum before going on to become Home Secretary with ideas about citizenship classes and tests for those people newly arrived in the United Kingdom. Statements by key advisers from the Qualifications and Curriculum Authority, such as the then chief executive Nick Tate, stressed the importance of what it means to be English at a time when a Scottish Parliament and Welsh Assembly were being established (Abrams, 1995). This emphasis on legal status in the national context tends to find easy expression in the form of citizenship education as opposed to other possible formulations of social and political education such as human rights education.

- Some feel the need to respond to a perceived decline in associational activity. Probably the most influential publication in this regard has been a book by Putnam (2000) titled *Bowling alone*. This refers principally to the American context and suggests that more people are less keen to work and undertake leisure activities with others. There are, however, concerns elsewhere. The low turnout in the 2001 general election in Britain has intensified longstanding debates about the levels of engagement of young people in the political process (e.g. Jowell and Park, 1997). It should be said that there is no widespread agreement that the voting figures are significantly lower for young people when compared with previous generations. Nor is there agreement that young people are alienated generally from the political process. There is a concern, however, that young people may be bored by politicians and there is the fear (by those politicians) that apathy and disengagement could develop in such a way as to promote instability. The emphasis in the National Curriculum documentation on the civil and criminal justice systems seem relevant here.

- It always seems likely that economic considerations are significant when aspects of social and political education are being modified. Part of the National Curriculum guidance for pupils aged 11–16 includes the need to understand 'economic institutions and systems that influence their lives and communities' and to learn about 'how the economy functions, including the role of business and financial services' (DfEE/QCA 1999, pp14–15). It would be far too crude to suggest that the citizenship education curriculum has been designed exclusively or even principally with the intention of developing the economic prosperity of the nation. However, it would be naïve to ignore the possibility that a key element of a preferred approach to citizenship would be to engender a notion of enterprise and to accept the economic responsibilities associated with the move towards the 'modernised' welfare state.

• The international and global aspects of citizenship are also key factors that are associated with the implementation of educational work. The first of the bullet points mentioned above drew attention to the significance of the national context in which legal status is highly important. It is not necessarily a contradiction to assert that at the same time there is a strong feeling that the reality of globalisation is being recognised. Throughout the National Curriculum documentation there are references to the diversity of identity. The national context is emphasised, but so is the 'world as a global community' and the 'wider issues of global interdependence and responsibility including sustainable development' (DfEE/QCA 1999, pp14–5).

The above four factors do not provide an exhaustive account of the rise of citizenship education. More needs to be said about the fundamental purposes of education and the precise circumstances in which citizenship education has been developed. However, as a thumbnail sketch of some of the key prompts to action they are, perhaps, a useful way of beginning to think about the sort of citizenship that is being promoted. This leads us to ask more directly about the nature of citizenship and citizenship education.

What is citizenship?

The above discussion about the causes of the implementation of citizenship education does not, of course, make clear what citizenship actually means. However, it would be unwise to suggest that a simple characterisation can be developed that would find widespread agreement. There is a danger that the citizenship debate becomes so all- embracing that it loses meaning altogether. Audigier (1998) has drawn the parameters of citizenship education so broadly that he has achieved both a reasonable position but an impossible target for teachers. He asserts:

> Since the citizen is an informed and responsible citizen, capable of taking part in public debate and making choices, nothing of what is human should be unfamiliar to him [sic], nothing of what is experienced in society should be foreign to democratic citizenship (p13)

That said, there must be some coherence and we would suggest that citizenship is, principally, about three inter-related matters. Firstly, a legal and political status that recognises rights and responsibilities. It is probably most useful here to use Marshall's well-known characterisation of civil (legal), political (franchise) and social (welfare) rights. Secondly, there are issues of identity that involve individual, local, national, global and other contexts. We may, legally, be British, but do we feel British? The issue of 'belongingness' is vital to educational initiatives in this field (Isin and Wood, 1999). Thirdly, citizens need to be able to participate. This means that it would be useful to attempt to ensure that appropriate knowledge and understanding, skills and dispositions were developed among citizens. If people are legally entitled to rights but are unable to take action to achieve them, then we are neglecting the importance of citizenship as it is experienced rather than how it is imagined.

Problematic issues

It is not possible in the space of a brief chapter to explore all the many characterisations of citizenship, but it is clear that the three-pronged framework given in the preceding section (legal status; identity; participation) gives rise immediately to a number of challenging issues. These problems are discussed by means of referring to one fundamental challenge and then by raising four examples of associated difficulties.

The fundamental issue can be addressed directly. Within the many debates about citizenship there are two distinct traditions. Heater (1999) refers to the civic republican and the liberal. Using very crude measures, it could be said that the former stresses duties in a public context; the latter emphasises rights to be exercised by individuals. Heater is confident about the possibility of these traditions being brought together:

> ... by being a virtuous, community conscious participant in civic affairs (a republican requirement), a citizen benefits by enhancing his or her own individual development (a liberal objective). Citizenship does not involve an either/or choice (p177).

McLaughlin (2001) develops this argument by suggesting that we should not stress the fragmentation that may appear to be an essential part of a diverse society:

> ... although we tend to think of 'diversity' and 'pluralism' as being concerned with difference and disagreement, it is important to note that both notions presuppose and require common values. Without significant values, ideals and procedures which are 'common' a diverse pluralist society would not only disintegrate but would also lack, among other things, such values as freedom, equality, a concern for evidence and reason, respect for persons and tolerance which are essential not only to liberal democracy but to the notions of 'diversity' and 'pluralism' themselves (p6).

We are clearly of the view that citizenship education can be a positive unifying force that is capable of being dynamic rather than static, vibrantly democratic as opposed to being narrowly hegemonic. However, the identification of those common values and traditions, the order of priority that we establish for them and the precise meaning that they have when we are engaged in the development of practical challenges lead us into very complex difficulties. Teachers of citizenship are faced with profound challenges on a daily basis.

The remaining four problems or challenges are linked to the above fundamental problem. Firstly, we need to consider who is perceived as the key recipient of citizenship education. We have moved, generally, from elitist to activist conceptions of citizenship (Sears, Clarke and Hughes, 1999). It seems, in the light of various national curricula providing common education, that an appropriately democratic approach has been established. It will nevertheless be important for evaluators of citizenship education programmes to remain vigilant as to the possibility that different lessons are being taught to or learned by different types of children. It will be a massive achievement if schools are to escape their socialising role that they have performed for so long. Much of what takes place in schools as young people become political could be described as aimed at preserving the status quo as well as attempting to transform society (Hahn, 1998). Secondly, the form of citizenship that is provided tends to vary along what can be described as a conceptual/geographical interface. Teachers are not merely altering their geographical focus if they decide to concentrate on European instead of national or global citizenship. Rather, a different form of citizenship comes into play. Of course, beyond the differences **between** notions of citizenship lie a variety of perspectives **within** each characterisation. Legal considerations, for example, can shade into what are largely matters of attitude and perspective. For example, when considering world citizenship Heater (1997) has described the following continuum:

Vague			Precise
Member of the human race	● Responsible for the condition of the planet	● Individual subject to moral law	● Promotion of world government

Thirdly, there are difficult practical challenges to face. It is now uncontroversial to assert that a key aim of citizenship is to encourage participation. Indeed the Crick Report that presaged the National Curriculum in England had very ambitious aims:

> We aim at no less than a change in the political culture of this country both nationally and locally; for people to think of themselves as active citizens, willing, able and equipped to have an influence in public life and with critical capacities to weigh

evidence before speaking and acting; to build on and to extend radically to young people the best in existing traditions of community involvement and public service and to make them individually confident in finding new forms of involvement and action among themselves. There are worrying levels of apathy, ignorance and cynicism about public life. These, unless tackled at every level, could well diminish the hoped for benefits both of constitutional reform and of the changing nature of the welfare state.

We have certainly gone well beyond giving any credence to views that apathy is somehow necessary for the efficient functioning of a democracy and so the above statement by Crick is to be welcomed. However, the nature of participation is often unspecified in such statements. There are obvious potential pitfalls, for example, to do with tokenism that leads to uncritical engagement in volunteering. It would be inappropriate if teachers became involved in a campaign that aimed merely at increasing voter turnout. The nature of participation needs to made explicit and broadened to ensure that abstaining from voting is seen as an example of deliberate indirect action. While uninterest is to be resisted, disinterest and even deliberate informed inactivity can be very useful in certain circumstances. Finally, we need to consider the relationship between the rise of citizenship education and the perception of a crisis in contemporary society. There has always been greater interest in political learning at times of crisis (Stradling 1987). Gollancz and Somervell (1914) and Stewart (1938) attracted attention at moments of crisis and were perceived as voices in the wilderness at other points. Currently there do not really seem to be many crisis cards to play and as such it may not easily be imagined what will sustain citizenship education in the long run. Furthermore, while sociologists such as Inglehart (1996) suggest that there is 'a gradual intergenerational shift toward placing less emphasis on respect for authority' (p661) and Blair (1995) asserts that 'duty is an essential Labour concept', the continuation of a quietist citizenship education remains a real possibility.

We had received a wealth of information from the French Music Bureau about Senegal, the experiences of Africans living in Paris (hugely interesting to our predominantly African pupils), and French language rap music. So we hosted a Senegalese rap group, Djoloff, for a day. Our school's steel pans gave an impromptu performance for our VIP visitors, and I almost wept with joy as they introduced themselves in French. The sight of these tall African rappers in national dress sitting eating lunch with our pupils has remained a talking point over the eighteen months since the visit, and prompted interest from the whole school in the video our French Club produced about the visit, which included interviews in French.

Charles Claxton, Head of MFL, Archbishop Ramsey Technology College, Camberwell, London

What is to be done?

In light of the discussion above, it would be unwise to suggest that citizenship education can be implemented in an easy and straightforward manner. However, there are successful projects for citizenship education in schools and elsewhere and we would like to outline one of these briefly here to highlight the positive outcomes of this kind of work.

An ongoing collaborative project is funded by the European Union and the Government of Canada with contributions from the British Council. It involves principally the exchange of student teachers between three Canadian provinces and three European countries (UK, Germany, Sweden) and aims to help prepare them to become effective teachers of citizenship education. The collaboration provides us with insights into some of the issues outlined in this chapter. Both Europe and Canada are good examples of the tensions (creative and otherwise) that arise from the many debates about citizenship, including those to do with political unification and uniformity or plurality of culture.

The aim is that the exchange will allow for a greater understanding among young people of the changing nature of citizenship, their rights and responsibilities as citizens, and the complexities of membership of different and sometimes conflicting contexts (from local to global), so that they can make informed decisions as future voters, workers, parents and community participants. It is hoped that, through the exchanges and workshops envisaged in the project, student teachers will be challenged to question and reflect upon the fundaments of citizenship, such as loyalty, patriotism, identity formation and forms of civic participation. They will encounter multiple perspectives on key national and global issues and trends, and they will be introduced to a variety of successful practices in education for citizenship as developed by the partner institutions.

Student teachers work in placement schools for six weeks where they learn about citizenship and teach it. Extra activities heighten their awareness of citizenship issues in Canada and Europe and students undertake small-scale research projects to investigate questions such as:

* What are the knowledge, skills of participation and dispositions toward citizenship of students and teachers you have met?

* What is the orientation toward citizenship represented in the official curriculum?

* How does citizenship education look on the ground – particularly when compared to the intended curriculum? Are there examples of best practice?

* How do these findings compare with citizenship education in your own country? What can be learned from your experience?

These student projects help to promote reflection on, and to make coherent, the multiple experiences that students encounter. They will also be accepted by the home institution as fulfilling a requirement for teacher certification. Throughout the project issues associated with language and culture will be very significant. The students from Germany and Sweden are facing most explicitly challenges to do with language. We want to ensure that all students are eligible to take part in the exchange but some may not apply to take part if they feel that their competence is not sufficient. There may also be some over confidence on the part of those who are already fluent in English but who may, as a result, assume that Canadian and European societies are more similar than they are in reality. Of course, we need to ensure that student teachers can function in the foreign country in which they will undertake their placement, but we need to ensure that opportunities for intercultural dialogue are taken by all. Early evaluation suggests that the project is helping to develop students' cultural horizons, including language skills, and their understanding and skills for citizenship education.

This outline does not do full justice to the project or to the hopes attached to it. It should perhaps be read merely as indication of our determination to encourage teachers to reflect on the complexities of citizenship, to look beyond narrow national considerations and to become effective actors and participants in bringing the benefits of citizenship education to others.

Conclusion

Citizenship education is a complex and controversial area. In this chapter we have drawn attention to a number of significant fundamental challenges that must be faced if the grand ambitions that are currently being asserted are to be realised. For all the problems that exist this is probably the best opportunity to develop citizenship education that has come about in at least a generation. We are trying, cautiously and tentatively, to seize the moment.

Bibliography

Abrams, F. (1995) 'How would you teach a child what it means to be English?', *Independent on Sunday*, 23 July, p6.

Arthur, J. and Wright, D. (2001) *Teaching citizenship in the secondary school*. David Fulton.

Audigier, F. (1998) *Basic concepts and core competences of education for democratic citizenship: an initial consolidated report*. Strasbourg: Council of Europe.

Blair, T. (1995) 'End the take and give away society'. In: *The Guardian*, 23 March.

Cogan, J. J. and Derricott, R. (1998) *Citizenship for the 21st century: an international perspective on education*. Kogan Page.

Crick, B. and Heater, D. (1977) *Essays on political education*. Falmer Press.

DfEE/QCA (1999) *Citizenship*. The National Curriculum for England. DfEE/QCA.

Davies, I. (1998) 'Citizenship education in Europe'. *Children's social and economics education* 3, 3, 127–140.

Davies, I. (1999) 'What has happened in the teaching of politics in schools in England in the last three decades, and why?' In: *Oxford Review of Education*, 25, 1 & 2, 125–140.

Doyé, P. (1996) 'Foreign language teaching and education for intercultural and international understanding'. In: *Evaluation and Research in Education*, 10, pp104–112.

Fogelman, K. (ed) (1991) *Citizenship in schools*. David Fulton.

Fouts, J. and Lee, W.O. (in press) *The meaning of citizenship*.

Gollancz, V. and Somervell, D. (1914) *Political education at a public school*. Collins.

Hahn, C. (1998) *Becoming political*. New York: SUNY.

Heater, D. (1999) *What is citizenship?* Polity Press.

Inglehart, R. (1996) 'Generational shifts in citizenship behaviours: the role of education and economic security in the declining respect for authority in industrial society.' In: *Prospects*, 26, pp653–662.

Isin, E. F. and Wood, P. K. (1999) *Citizenship and identity*. Sage.

Jowell, R. and Park, A. (1997) *Young people, politics and citizenship – a disengaged generation?* Paper delivered at the *Citizenship foundation annual colloquium*. Citizenship Foundation.

McLaughlin, T. (2001) *Ethos and example in social and moral development in the school*. Paper presented to the conference *The social and moral fabric of the school*, Institute for Learning, University of Hull, September 6–8, 2001.

Putnam, R. D. (2000) *Bowling alone: the collapse and revival of American community*. New York: Simon and Schuster.

Sears, A., Clarke G. M. and Hughes, A. (1999) 'Canadian citizenship education: the pluralist ideal and citizenship education for a post-modern state'. In: Torney-Purta, J., Schwille, J. and Amadeo, J-A. (1999) *Civic education across countries: twenty-four national case studies from the IEA Civic Education Project*. Amsterdam: The International Association for the Evaluation of Educational Achievement.

Stewart, M. (1938) *Bias and education for democracy*. Oxford University Press.

Stradling, R. and Noctor, M. (1981) *The provision of political education*. Curriculum Review Unit.

Stradling, R. (1987) *Political education and political socialisation in Britain: a ten-year retropsective*. Paper presented at the *International round table conference of the research committee on political education of the International Politica Science Association,* Ostkolleg der Bundeszentrale für Politische Bildung, Köln, March 9–13.

Torney-Purta, J., Schwille, J. and Amadeo, J-A. (1999) *Civic education across countries: twenty-four national case studies from the IEA Civic Education Project*. Amsterdam: The International Association for the Evaluation of Educational Achievement.

White, C., Bruce, S. and Ritchie, J. (2000) *Young people's politics. Political interest and engagement amongst 14 to 24 year olds*. Joseph Rowntree Foundation.

Chapter 5

Citizenship and community languages: a critical perspective

Jim Anderson and Manju Chaudhuri

Jim Anderson and Manju Chaudhuri look at citizenship education and community languages. Their practical examples illustrate how teaching and learning in community language classrooms can go well beyond learning about language structure and make explicit to pupils social and intercultural issues which are central to citizenship education.

Breaking the wall of silence

The relationship between community languages[1] and citizenship in the curriculum is potentially rich and thought-provoking as we shall seek to show in this chapter, but it is also problematic and it would be both misleading and dishonest not to make this clear from the outset. Rather than seeing the presence of diverse cultures and languages within British society as something to be valued and supported, the continual thrust of British education policy has been the emphasis on acquisition of English and the implication that time devoted to other languages will inevitably undermine this process as well as being potentially divisive socially (Swann, 1985). Thus curriculum-based bilingual education in this country is limited to the Celtic communities in Wales, Scotland and Northern Ireland as well as a few programmes involving major European languages. The National Curriculum, in fact, offers no support for the development of community languages at primary level, and at secondary level the only basis for their inclusion is under the umbrella of Modern **Foreign** Languages. The assimilationist intent is clear, therefore, and is further reflected in the fact that no government records are kept of what languages are currently being studied and by how many students in mainstream schools. It is evident, however, that the majority of community language teaching is taking place not within mainstream schools, but in classes usually run at the weekend and organised by community groups. In London alone, where a recent survey has identified more than 300 different languages (Baker and Eversley, 2000), it is known that over 500 such classes exist (Kempadoo and Abdelrazak, 2001).

The question that arises, therefore, is to what extent mainstream schools are aware of this work going on in the community and to what extent the linguistic and cultural expertise of students attending such schools is recognised and valued by the mainstream school? The common impression is that schools are pleased to enter bilingual students for public examinations in their home language(s) because results achieved boost exam performance tables, but that beyond this very little encouragement or support is provided and very little thought given to ways in which the linguistic and intercultural skills involved could be used as a resource to enhance the learning of all students. By default, if not by design, these voices in their diversity and richness have effectively been stifled. Within the theoretical framework developed by the French sociologist Pierre Bourdieu (1991), the experience and expertise that bilingual students bring into school is seen to have minimal, if any, value because it does not relate to the kind of 'cultural capital' which has currency in schools. In other words, it is not part of what counts as knowledge.

Clearly this issue goes right to the heart of what in social, cultural and educational terms we understand by the term 'inclusion'. In a pertinent analysis, Batelaan and Van Hoof (1996: 6) set out the options facing multicultural societies (see Table 1 below):

Options for multicultural societies

The intercultural option	The monocultural option
Pluralism based on human rights which are inclusive	Nationalism and fundamentalism, based on superiority, exclusive rights
Interdependence, which requires mutual understanding, based on shared values	Apartheid, separatism leading to suppression, ethnic purity, racism, based on group values
Equal opportunities	Protection of privileges of the own group

Table 1

If citizenship is to espouse 'pluralist' values in a meaningful way, then it must recognise (a) that every language represents a unique and precious expression of culture, (b) that languages form an integral part of a person's identity, their sense of who they are and where they come from (c) that being able to relate to more than one of the many languages (and indeed dialects) spoken in Britain does not make a person less British.

As Campbell (2000: 32) points out:

> *In culturally diverse societies, the phenomenon of belonging to more than one cultural group and moving between such groups is no longer unusual. It is possible to wear the badge of civic symbols of cultural identity such as citizenship, while at the same time identifying with one or more specific cultural groups within the nation ... These cultural identities are not mutually exclusive, but cumulative layers, where the immediate cultural context determines which layer is relevant at any particular time ...*

Moreover, this should not be a cause of shame or nostalgia for some mythical notion of cultural or ethnic purity. We should be celebrating the fact that we are well placed to prepare young people for a world in which, as recent reports clearly recognise (Centre for Education for Racial Equality in Scotland, 1999; Scottish Executive, 2000; Nuffield Languages Inquiry, 2000; Centre for Information on Language Teaching and Research, 2001), the need is for intercultural literacy comprising both language skills (and not just in European languages) and the ability to navigate cultural difference. As Campbell (ibid: 37) puts it:

> *The ability to adapt quickly and effectively to unfamiliar cultural environments is becoming one of the key skills demanded by an internationalised economy and rapidly changing domestic social contexts. In a society characterised by social and cultural change, neither our students nor our teachers can afford to remain culturally encapsulated.*

As we move on to look at how community languages ´fit into the National Curriculum framework for citizenship, it will become clear just how strong the links are. It should also be borne in mind, however, that there is very little explicit recognition of this in official documentation (QCA, 1998, 2000, 2001; DfEE/QCA,1999).

How much do you and your colleagues know about the community languages spoken by students in your school?

- Find a way to conduct a survey to raise awareness of the linguistic richness and diversity in your school.

- Discuss with your colleagues ways in which you might build on the expertise of students in your language teaching.

Community languages and citizenship in the context of the National Curriculum

Strikingly, community languages have important contributions to make both to issues of equality and diversity within British society (an inward looking perspective) and to understanding our role and responsibilities within the global community (an outward looking perspective). In the National Curriculum Programme of Study for Citizenship, Part 1 (see Table 2 below), Statement 1.b (common at Key Stages 3 and 4) relates clearly to the former of these perspectives and Statements 1.i (KS3) and 1.i and 1.j (KS4) to the latter.

Knowledge and understanding about becoming informed citizens

KS3 Pupils should be taught about:	KS4 Pupils should be taught about:
1.b the diversity of national, regional, religious and ethnic identities in the United Kingdom and the need for mutual respect and understanding	**1.b** the origins and implications of the diverse national, regional, religious and ethnic identities in the United Kingdom and the need for mutual respect and understanding
1.i the world as a global community, and the political, economic, environmental and social implications of this, and the role of the European Union, the Commonwealth and the United Nations.	**1.i** the United Kingdoms' relations in Europe, including the European Union, and relations with the Commonwealth and the United Nations.
	1.j the wider issues and challenges of global interdependence and responsibility, including sustainable development and Local Agenda 21.

Table 2: Extract from the National Curriculum Programme of Study for Citizenship (Section 1)

There are clear links here with Part 4 of the NC/MFL Programme of Study, entitled 'Developing cultural awareness', in which learning to compare cultures and to explore issues from different cultural perspectives are seen as essential elements. There is also an obvious connection to the section of the National Curriculum document for MFL entitled 'About modern foreign languages in the National Curriculum', one part of which is devoted to 'Promoting pupils' spiritual, moral, social and cultural development through MFL'. Finally, it is worth mentioning at this point the section in the National Curriculum devoted to inclusion, in particular Part B of 'Responding to pupils' diverse learning needs', which recognises the importance of planning work which builds on students' interests and cultural experiences.

The Citizenship Programme of Study (Parts 2 and 3) make clear that the way students should acquire 'knowledge and understanding about becoming informed citizens' is through developing skills of 'enquiry and communication', and 'participation and responsible action'. The rationale here is that young people are most likely to engage meaningfully with ideas and commit to values and attitudes when they experience them as part of the way they learn and interact with each other in the school community. As Brownlie (2001: 14) points out:

> *The way in which citizenship is taught and pupils learn conveys, either explicitly or implicitly, messages about involvement in society. It can say as much, if not more, to pupils about global citizenship than any subject matter.*

Again there are clear links with the MFL Programme of Study. There is a common emphasis on active learning within meaningful contexts, on working with others, on researching via a range of resources, on developing independence and creativity, on the construction of knowledge through a process orientation. The extra dimension that the citizenship curriculum brings to this is that of decision making and action, i.e. personal involvement in the democratic process. Brownlie's analysis (ibid: 14) of the five stages towards participative and experiential learning, set out below, makes this point clear:

(i) Pupils become aware
(ii) Pupils become more informed
(iii) Pupils develop their understanding
(iv) Pupils develop their own views and opinions
(v) Pupils take action

What citizenship offers is an opportunity to engage with a range of issues that are often overlooked in MFL lessons, partly as a result of the GCSE specification which tends to trivialise content or message in favour of an emphasis on medium. Clearly, where students are operating at low levels of proficiency in the target language, there are pedagogical challenges in enabling them to engage meaningfully with serious issues such as terrorism or racism or the effects of famine. For students of community languages, however, although literacy skills may be underdeveloped, especially when dealing with a non-Roman script as in the case of Bengali, listening and speaking skills are generally high and this means that it is a lot easier to tackle such issues. The teacher can draw on students' abilities in oral and aural skills to generate whole class and group discussions and at the same time provide support for literacy development by noting key words and ideas on the board. When it comes to activities involving reading and writing, differentiated support will usually be required. Although it is important that students have the opportunity to develop all four skills as they carry out their work, it is also appropriate that in performing specific tasks individual strengths and weaknesses are taken into account. This may involve some students initially making oral rather than written contributions. An example here would be students with low level literacy skills being assigned recorded interviews as their major contribution.

Different levels of support will be needed, but the important point is that students should become involved in cognitively challenging work. If the study of the community language is to be seen by students as stimulating and worth pursuing as a subject, it is essential that content moves beyond the transactional needs of the tourist or describing the events of the previous weekend. They need to engage with culture at a deeper level, to understand that the heritage they possess from their country of origin is one to be proud of, one that can enrich their lives and make them feel whole as human beings. This is not to argue, incidentally, for some monolithic notion of culture feeding into separate and fixed identities. The typical pattern that is emerging ever more clearly is one of hybridity (Gilroy, 1987; Mercer, 1994; Hall; 1988, 1992; Rampton, 1995) in which influences from different cultures are feeding into each other and where identities are being redefined. Young people growing up between cultures need the space to share and make sense of the different influences on their lives. This is a complex, but important and enriching process.

In the next section we provide examples of tasks designed for the secondary Bengali classroom, which both in terms of topic and pedagogical approach contribute to the citizenship curriculum.

Citizenship in the community languages classroom

Brocklesby and Chaudhuri's (1998) *Bengali Manual* provides a useful model of what citizenship might look like in practice in the community languages classroom, or within the context of cross-curricular work. The booklet sets out to address the need for teaching resources which are not narrowly focused on language development, but which have important social and intercultural dimensions and which involve students in democratic decision-making processes. We would like to stress that, although the material referred to here relates to the teaching of Bengali, it could easily be adapted for other languages. The same themes and approaches would apply equally well to the teaching of Chinese, Arabic and Turkish for example.

Three assignments are proposed in the booklet. These are:

1. Planning a visit to Bangladesh

The brief requires students to plan a two-week visit to Bangladesh for a group of young people and their leaders, bearing in mind that the visitors:

(a) do not speak Bengali;
(b) know very little about Bangladesh;
(c) will be staying with families;
(d) do not have a lot of money.

The outcomes they work towards are the creation and presentation of information packs.

2. School in Bangladesh and Britain

The brief is a comparative study of education in Bangladesh and Britain leading up to the creation of a display, a game or a drama sketch.

3. Planning a youth conference

The brief is to plan a one-day conference for 200 Bengali speakers aged 14–18 at a suitable local meeting place. One or more themes may be debated at the conference and among those suggested are International Women's Day, Nobel prize winners of the year, the environment, terrorism, AIDS and HIV and child labour.

Instructions are also given as to how the projects should be carried out and the three following features emerge as central to each:

* collaborative group work (involving self-assessment);
* investigative research;
* presentation to an audience.

COLLABORATIVE GROUP WORK

The assignments require students to work together to solve problems and achieve goals and to work with a range of classmates, not just their friends. Groupings are decided by the teacher to ensure a balance of abilities and, if appropriate, a mix of genders. Although the broad aim of assignments is defined, groups can choose the content and form that their work takes. There are times when teacher input is essential, to talk through the aims and objectives of the assignment and to monitor and comment on progress as the project proceeds. An important element of group work is the development of management and leadership skills, and group organisers are expected to chair discussions within the group, to allocate tasks, to set time limits and to record progress.

INVESTIGATIVE RESEARCH

In each assignment students are expected to access and evaluate information from a range of resources including:

* documents (texts, photographs, web pages);
* interview data;
* audio and video recordings;
* field notes;
* diaries.

The Internet offers a vast range of up-to-date resources on a wide range of topics and the possibility of a virtual tour of Bangladesh, for example, to visit schools and discover how the education system works there or to find out about famous people. Where a link has been established with a school in Bangladesh, the assignment can be carried out in both schools. Communication can take place via e-mail with outcomes being published on the Web for a global audience[2]. Cummins and Sayers (1995) argue persuasively that such projects can provide a powerful means of developing global awareness and ultimately of challenging cultural illiteracy. On a more modest scale students can be encouraged to write to family and friends in Bangladesh and ask them to send information and photographs.

PRESENTATION TO AN AUDIENCE

Each of the assignments proposed in the *Bengali manual* involves students in presentations to an audience which may be the class group with invited guest(s) or another class or could be an event for an open day or parents' evening. This makes the process more meaningful to students and also fosters a sense of responsibility, self-confidence and respect for different viewpoints. It takes an act of courage to present yourself to an audience, to make your voice heard, to expose yourself to potential criticism, but it is also exciting and empowering.

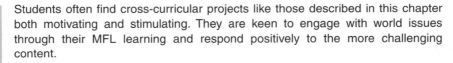

Students often find cross-curricular projects like those described in this chapter both motivating and stimulating. They are keen to engage with world issues through their MFL learning and respond positively to the more challenging content.

- Take one of the projects outlined here and adapt it for your students. You might choose a theme linked to GCSE topics, such as tourism (see page 2) or child labour (pocket money) or water (house and home). Ask pupils to work in groups both in class and for homework and to give presentations to the class in the language they are learning.

- Evaluate the project with students and discuss their responses with colleagues. How might you approach a project like this again?

For more examples and photocopiable resources see:

Brown, K. and Brown, M. (1998) ResourceFile 1: *Changing places.* CILT.

The assignments in practice

A range of positive outcomes were identified when these assignments were piloted with mixed ability Year 10 Bengali classes in several inner city secondary schools. Students welcomed the opportunity to explore issues which gave them a deeper understanding of Bengali culture and drew on their experience at home and in their community as well on their links with schools in Bangladesh.

The assignments helped to develop students' global awareness with regard, for example, to differences in educational opportunities for people living in rich and poor countries. One group produced a set of photographs with captions illustrating differences between schools in Bangladesh and Britain. Students commented on how much people living here take for granted such as free education. They were struck by the difficulties many young people in poorer countries face as a result of poverty and this led them to reflect on questions of equality and justice. There was a visible shift in attitudes. Interestingly, the assignment also led students to ask whether they might arrange a class trip to Bangladesh.

However, while deepening appreciation of some of the difficulties faced by the majority of people living in Bangladesh, it was also clear that the assignments gave students a sense of pride in their cultural heritage. Thus in the first assignment, students were able to celebrate the richness of the land and the culture, drawing on information, photographs and other documents from family members and friends and sometimes on personal experience of travel to Bangladesh. In the third assignment, one class focused on International Women's Day and mounted a bilingual display in the school library celebrating world famous women of past and present from Eastern as well as Western backgrounds. Colleagues commented on how it helped to challenge sexist and racist stereotypes and on its positive effect in increasing confidence and self-respect especially among Asian girls. It led, among other things, to students expressing the wish to find out about other women of achievement living within their local community.

What stood out from the assignments was the sense of empowerment that students gained not only in terms of recognition of identity and culture, but also of an ability to engage in democratic, decision-making processes. Feedback from students at the end of the assignments was overwhelmingly positive and a number expressed the wish to be allowed to undertake similar assignments in future Bengali lessons.

It is not suggested, however, that there were no difficulties involved in enabling students to work much more autonomously. It can take some time for students to get used to working in this way. Students need to understand their different roles and responsibilities and appreciate the importance of communicating as much as possible in standard Bengali. They also need to be aware that these are important assessment criteria alongside the quality of the outcomes. The difference in levels of literacy has important implications for the kind of texts and support sheets that teachers need to have available. For all of these reasons teachers should not launch into assignments of this type without careful preparation or without exploring the potential for collaboration with colleagues working in other curriculum areas.

Resolving contradictions

In this chapter we have sought to demonstrate the unique contribution that community languages can make to meeting the new requirements for citizenship in the National Curriculum. We have seen how the kind of assignments proposed in the *Bengali manual* enable students to involve themselves in work which takes account of identity and culture as well as language and which promotes active participation in decision- making processes. We have also seen how such work can feed into cross-curricular projects and provide a context for all students to learn to engage with otherness, to develop respect for other cultures and to look upon different experiences and perspectives not as a threat, but as an enrichment.

The question is what scope schools will provide for such transformative pedagogy to be implemented, for inevitably it challenges existing relations of power operating in society and reflected in educational policy. The essential choice is between the monocultural and intercultural options identified in the introduction to this chapter. We cannot pretend to subscribe to pluralist values on the one hand while perpetuating a discriminatory, if not racist, language policy on the other.

As Batelaan and Van Hoof (ibid: 7) point out:

> *Issues of diversity and inequality are two sides of the same coin. It is impossible to combat inequality without valuing diversity. On the other hand, it does not make much sense to accentuate 'diversity' in festivals or in an exotic curriculum without real concern about existent inequalities.*

Bibliography

Baker, P. and Eversley, J. (eds) (2000) *Multilingual capital*. Battlebridge Publications.

Batelaan, P. and Van Hoof, C. (1996) 'Cooperative learning in intercultural education'. In: *European Journal of Intercultural Studies*, 7: 3.

Bourdieu, P. (1991) *Language and symbolic power*. Polity Press.

Brocklesby, C. and Chaudhuri, M. (1998) *Bengali manual*. London: Language Support Service, Tower Hamlets Professional Development Centre.

Brownlie, A. (2001) *Citizenship education: the global dimension. Guidance for Key Stages 3 and 4*. Development Education Association.

Campbell, A. (2000) 'Cultural identity as a social construct'. In: *Intercultural Education*, 11: 1.

Centre for Education for Racial Equality in Scotland (1999) *Bilingualism, community languages and Scottish education: a challenge for policy makers and practitioners in a devolved Scotland*. CERES.

Centre for Information on Language Teaching and Research (2001) *An agenda for languages*. CILT.

Cummins, J. and Sayers, D. (1995) *Brave new schools – challenging cultural illiteracy through global learning networks.* New York: St Martin's Press.

DfEE/QCA (1999) Citizenship: The National Curriculum for England. QCA.

Gilroy, P. (1987) *There ain't no black in the Union Jack.* Routledge.

Hall, S. (1988) New ethnicities. *ICA Documents* 7: 27–31.

Hall, S. (1992) 'The question of cultural identity'. In: Hall, S., Held, D. and McGrew, T. (eds) *Modernity and its futures.* Polity Press/Open University, 274–316.

Kempadoo and Abdelrazak (eds) (2001) *Directory of supplementary and mother-tongue classes* (2nd edn). Resource Unit for Supplementary and Mother-tongue Schools.

Mercer, K. (1994) *Welcome to the jungle.* Routledge.

The Nuffield Foundation (2000) *Languages: the next generation. The final report and recommendations of the Nuffield Languages Inquiry.* The English Company (UK) Ltd.

QCA (1998) *Education for citizenship and the teaching of democracy in schools: Final report of the Advisory Group on Citizenship.* QCA.

QCA (2000) *Citizenship at Key Stages 3 and 4: Initial guidance for schools.* QCA.

QCA (2001) *Citizenship: a scheme of work for Key Stage 3.* QCA.

Rampton, B. (1995) *Crossing: language and ethnicity among adolescents.* Longman.

Scottish Executive (2000) *Citizens of a multilingual world: Key issues.* Scottish Executive.

Scottish Executive (2000) *Citizens of a multilingual world: rationale.* Scottish Executive.

Scottish Executive (2000) *Citizens of a multilingual world: recommendations.* Scottish Executive.

Swann, M. (1985) *Education for all: the report of the Committee of inquiry into the education of children from ethnic minority groups.* HMSO.

Notes

1 'Community languages' is the term that has come to be used most widely in the UK to describe those languages which are used by ethnic minority communities. They are languages, in other words, towards which users, whatever their level of competence, experience an emotional attachment and which form a part of their heritage and thus of their identity. Patterns of use of community languages vary considerably within families, partly because some parents believe (sometimes on the basis of misinformation provided by teachers) that development of the first language will hamper the child's development in English. Typically, proficiency in the language decreases across generations and this is even more likely to happen where, as in the UK, prevailing social and political attitudes, reflected in educational policy, are unfavourable. This applies particularly to literacy which represents an important stage in language development and may be crucial in attaining high-level bilingual competence. It is also important to note that the language spoken within a certain community may not be the standard form of the language. Thus the majority of settlers

from Bangladesh speak Sylheti dialect (which has no written tradition) rather than the standard Bengali which students need to acquire in order to pass examinations. The picture is a complex one and likely to become more so through the trend towards mixings of languages and the redefinition of the cultural landscape which this implies.

A useful introduction to the broad range of linguistic diversity in the UK can be found on the British Council website at: **www.britishcouncil.org/multilingualuk/**

2 Projects/organisations promoting on-line partnerships of this type include:

Windows on the World
Windows on the World is a database for schools and colleges seeking partner institutions anywhere in the world in order to develop international education projects. The site is managed by the Central Bureau for International Education and Training. In WOTW showcase there is information about a range of projects linking schools in the UK with others world wide. In many cases, including those involving schools in India and China, communication is maintained via the Internet. Case studies are featured in the 'showcase' section of the site.
www.wotw.org.uk

Montage*plus*
An initiative of the British Council in Australia **Montage*plus*** is a series of stimulating interactive curriculum projects, a teaching resource and a means of creating virtual communities of students and teachers around the world!

The projects are designed to develop and maintain collaboration between participants using the latest information communications technology (ICT) which motivates students and creates more effective learning. Students become involved in real-life situations involving communication, collaboration, self-directed learning, problem solving, research and the publication of findings
www.montageplus.co.uk/about/index.htm

Intercultural E-Mail Classroom Connections – P/S
IECC (Intercultural E-Mail Classroom Connections) is a free service to help teachers link with partners in other countries and cultures for e-mail classroom pen-pal and project exchanges. Since its creation in 1992, IECC has distributed over 28,000 requests for e-mail partnerships. At last count, more than 7650 teachers in 82 countries were participating in one or more of the IECC lists.
www.iecc.org

Internet Learning Trust
The Internet Learning Trust is a British educational charity working to ensure more equal access to learning opportunities through innovative use of ICT. One project has linked five schools in Soweto, South Africa with five in Birmingham. Details of this can be found on the website. The aim now is to develop further web based projects in South Africa, but also in India, Jamaica, Botswana and many other countries
www.netschools.org/index.html

The Alliance for Global Learning
The Alliance for Global Learning is a strategic partnership between Schools Online, World Links for Development (WorLD), and the International Education and Resource Network (I*EARN). An unprecedented consortium, the Alliance for Global Learning,

was created to address inequity and provide education opportunities through technology for more students around the world.
www.global-learning.org/en/index.php3

Projects using Information and Communications Technology (PICT)
PICT schools are making active use of Information and Communications Technologies in their projects. This site celebrates their success and seeks to assist other schools wanting to make more use of ICT in their international projects.

PICT involves schools in the UK, Ireland, France, the Netherlands, Lithuania and Slovakia, engaged in European Education Projects with partners in at least two other European countries. **The site contains valuable information on the different technologies involved.**
www.europict.org

Chapter 6

Citizenship and modern foreign languages in the primary school

Ann Gregory with Sally Hicks and Therese Comfort

The authors of this chapter draw on their experiences of planning and carrying out cross-curricular projects with primary-aged pupils to show how citizenship and language learning can work together. They argue that primary teachers have a special role to play in encouraging positive attitudes in younger pupils towards cultural and linguistic difference and give practical examples of resources they developed to support pupils' learning about citizenship.

The framework for Personal, Social and Health Education (PSHE) and Citizenship at Key Stages 1 and 2 was introduced into schools in 2000 as a non-statutory area, although in Key Stages 3 and 4 it has become statutory from September 2002. Modern Foreign Languages (MFL) are currently taught to 20–25% of primary-age pupils (CILT 2001) and recent announcements indicate a growth in this area of the curriculum (www.nacell.org.uk). The authors of this chapter argue that the links between issues of citizenship and foreign language teaching are closely interwoven. Younger pupils can be very receptive to issues involved in citizenship education and to the nature of linguistic and cultural difference. This chapter will consider the particular opportunities that the primary school environment offers for linking different areas of the curriculum, for developing an awareness of democracy and the role that MFL has to play in making these connections. Specific reference will be made to a project on *La Réunion*, focusing on the QCA MFL Schemes of Work for Key Stage 2, and a description of a project that is being planned to link primary schools in Morocco and York. Finally, some general comments will be made about ways in which, even in a crowded primary curriculum, citizenship and foreign languages can be linked.

The primary environment

In recent years primary schools have had to respond to a range of new initiatives, including the Literacy and Numeracy Strategies. It has often been difficult to find extra time in the curriculum for subjects such as MFL or creative and performing arts. However, many schools **have** found a way of broadening children's experience, often by 'killing two birds with one stone'. Whereas in secondary schools teachers tend to be specialists in one particular subject, it is most common in primary schools to find the generalist class teacher covering all areas of the curriculum.

The 'compartmentalisation' of the curriculum does not exist in most primary schools in the same way. Occasionally teachers will 'swop' classes to maximise teachers' expertise, and this may be the case for foreign languages, but on the whole one teacher is responsible for teaching one class for a year and for the development of individuals in the class. The primary teacher therefore has more time to get to know each child in her class and is able to value and encourage individual strengths. He or she is likely to be aware at an early stage of particular problems such as illness, anxiety or bullying and is able to deal with these immediately, often by involving the whole class in a discussion or announcement. During registration, in class-time or school assembly and during the valuable 'sharing' or 'carpet' time, the primary teacher can get the class together to deal with problems. Many secondary teachers, under pressure to cover the syllabus and to achieve high GCSE grades, might consider the idea of taking 'time out' of a lesson in this way unacceptable.

The primary approach has clear advantages for the development of citizenship in a natural way. Many primary schools operate class or school councils where children have a real voice in decisions which affect them, for example, how money raised by parents might be spent, or how to deal with litter. Some schools operate a 'friendship club', run by pupils, to help new pupils to settle more quickly into the school community. Others hold poster competitions to encourage social responsibility and many schools involve their pupils in planning festivals and concerts, performances for local elderly people, or charity collections for disaster funds.

Primary children can be more open and inquisitive than some older pupils. They can be more ready to accept differences than to criticise them. Lambert and Klineberg (1967) identified ten as the most receptive age for the introduction of cultural differences. Schumann (1978) suggested:

> It is at this age (10) that children are more likely to view foreign (sic) people as different, but at the same time interesting. After the age of ten (and often before it) children tend to associate 'different' with 'bad'.

Hawkins (1981) states that the capacity of many children for empathy, or their ability to see the world from someone else's point of view, is at its height around the age of nine, but declines rapidly with the onset of adolescence. After the onset of puberty, he suggests, attitudes become increasingly fixed, and it is more difficult to tackle issues of difference.

Teaching styles of many primary schools also facilitate the explicit linking of different curriculum areas. Despite recent trends towards more subject-specialist teaching, 'topic work', where several curriculum areas are linked, still has a visible presence in primary classrooms. For example, the history topic 'Tudors' can include creative writing, art work, maths, design-technology, dance, drama, and even science and foreign languages. This particular theme might also include debate on roles and responsibilities within families, or the impact of decisions and actions on future events, covering in this way PSHE and citizenship requirements.

The class teacher in the primary situation also has more autonomy than her secondary counterpart in the choice of materials used to deliver different aspects of the curriculum. The secondary teacher of English may be obliged to study particular set texts within a given range, whereas a primary teacher may be able to reflect pupils' interests and select a current best seller for shared enjoyment in class story-time. He or she may also choose which country or community to study as a 'distant location' theme for Key Stage 2 geography. Many primary schools include a 'year trip' or outdoor pursuits week for Year 6 pupils, and some schools are choosing the added benefits of a visit to a European country, where pupils are able to experience first-hand a different culture, language and people.

All of these examples show how citizenship, linked to other primary curriculum areas, can be presented to children in an integrated and 'natural' way.

A group of pupils investigating child labour in Guatemala devised questions and practised interview techniques and how to use a dictaphone. They took photographs and interviewed about ten children: Alfredo and Marcos Antonio, two twelve year old shoe shine boys; Lorenza (12) a fruit seller working under a busy flyover; Florinda (10) who sells chewing gum outside the immigration office and Marta (10) who sells hot tortillas from a basket. They discovered that some of these children had worked from as young as seven years old. They were working an average of 10–12 hours a day, six or even seven days a week. They worked to help their parents and consequently all of the money they earn goes to their parents, although some are lucky to keep 5 or 10 Quetzales (50p–£1.00) a day. The majority of the children interviewed still managed to go to school. They could only attend classes in the evening, after a hard day's work so often fell behind or were forced to drop out.

Taken from *Voces Españolas* project (see page 36)

KS2 QCA Schemes of Work for MFL, Unit 12

The QCA Schemes of Work for MFL for KS2 were produced in 2000 and provide twelve units of work to support foreign language teaching at KS2. The folder can be obtained, on request, from the QCA. Currently the Schemes of Work are non-statutory. The final unit (12) was developed as a revision and consolidation of the work proposed in the preceding eleven units, and was set in a distant location, a francophone country. Working with this theme, pupils can use their imagination and creativity to link other curriculum areas to the study of a foreign language in an authentic situation. The unit was also planned as a possible bridge between feeder primary schools and their secondary school, so that pupils might work together on a topic which could culminate in a joint celebration of language learning at the KS2/3 transfer point. It is acknowledged that the issue of continuity and progression between the two phases is one of the most challenging 'problems' when foreign languages are introduced in primary schools. It was suggested, for example, that even pupils in schools with foreign language teaching would be able to investigate the topic in English, and take part in a joint display or performance.

The focus of Unit 12 is teaching and revising the foreign language through the study of other curriculum areas. As will be seen in the description of the *La Réunion* and *Morocco* projects which follow, this might include the study of any other primary subject, such as geography, maths, creative writing, music, citizenship and PSHE. It is just as easy to present the foreign language element through a more distant and 'different' country as it is to present it through topic work on France or England. The 'differences' act as a stimulus for creativity, and the teacher can introduce as much language work as is appropriate for her pupils.

Curriculum 2000 is perceived by many primary teachers to have placed additional strains on the timetable, reducing flexibility and innovation. Constraints do exist for primary curriculum leaders and there are some moves towards compartmentalising subject areas on the secondary model. There **is** pressure on the curriculum and it was in response to this that the following project was developed.

La Réunion project

The original idea of preparing and trialling a pack of materials based on the French Département d'Outre Mer of la Réunion was the result of a series of happy coincidences. Through staff visits under the Erasmus Higher Education student mobility scheme, lecturers in French, drama and education from York St John College had opportunities to visit this small volcanic island in the Indian Ocean. Over a period of two years we began to build a collection of photographs, not of traditional tourist views, but of the everyday lives of primary-age children – at school, in the street, in the market, playing sport, doing homework, in the kitchen helping their mothers and so on. There were also photographs of the island itself, its volcano, the traffic, the mosques, the Hindu and Chinese temples, the vegetation, the cafés, the French post boxes, and a photograph of a duellist's grave and a pirate's tomb. In addition, a series of ordnance survey maps made a large wall display of the island. There were also 35 individual pieces of lava from the volcano (primary-age children benefit from learning through all the senses, touch, taste and smell as well as sight and sound), a plastic statue of the island's patron saint, some local recipes, a bus timetable and postcards, posters and tourist leaflets, and a CD of Sega music, which is the traditional Creole song and dance music of La Réunion. Filming had been arranged in a primary school in La Réunion and pupils of different ethnic origins introduced themselves and their families on camera in simple French. These materials formed the basis of the project.

Initially, it was envisaged that a 'topic pack' would support the study of 'the distant location' in KS2 geography and introduce an element of 'global awareness' to lessons, as well as providing authentic resources for the study of French. In discussion with teachers, it soon became apparent that the focus could be widened to include a reinforcement of other curriculum areas through the study of the foreign language. Some of the preparatory work was done in English, but much was achieved in French, through careful planning and clear focus of vocabulary and structure. Enlarging the colour photos and producing OHTs provided ready-made authentic flashcards, and of course computer images from digital cameras can now be used. Imaginative teaching gave the children a simulated plane journey to La Réunion, passing over, for example, *la France, le Sahara, le Madagascar*. Passports, completed in simple French, were produced at *'la Douane'*, and French language sessions, based on the photo pack, revised and consolidated what pupils had previously learnt in an 'English' context. In role plays they exchanged questions with 'Réunionnais pupils' based on the video: their names and ages, where they lived, their pets, families, likes and dislikes.

Pupils found out about the weather, the volcano, local festivals, food and drink, and religion sometimes in English, sometimes in French. They were quick to spot similarities, as well as differences, and were always curious and eager for more information – the desire to find out came from them rather than from their teacher. They asked to taste tropical fruit, made a *salade des fruits exotiques* and planned items to send in a shoe box to a class in La Réunion which would represent their life in Yorkshire (Jones, 1995). These included a photograph of a group of pupils meeting the Queen, some Harrogate toffee and a school tie.

After initial trials, other teachers took the materials and added to the activities. One class learnt some Sega dances, another re-enacted their version of the duel. The potential for map work, both in English and the target language was exploited. Several pupils were sufficiently stimulated by Internet searches at school to bring in information they had printed off at home, about sea shells and shark attacks. In one class, photographs of the many different shrines and temples formed the basis for a discussion about religious harmony. The introduction of PSHE and citizenship guidelines encouraged teachers to add this dimension to the range of existing curriculum possibilities.

One class was shown where La Réunion was on a globe and asked to imagine what life would be like there. They listed their ideas and the things they wanted to find out, then went on a physical 'trip' around the outside of the school, passing classrooms labelled 'La Belgique', 'La Suisse', 'L'Eygpte', and so on. Back outside their own room (now La Réunion), they went through 'Customs' and then 'got on a coach trip'. They entered the room in silence, and just by looking at the 'evidence' (photographs around the room) they were instructed to find out if their predictions about the island were *vrai ou faux*. Some well-travelled pupils were quite close in their predictions, while others were surprised to see computers like their own, buses and Coca-Cola signs. They noticed the houses represented both wealth and poverty, they were interested in the pictures of food, of class-rooms and the colourful dress. They had predicted a hot climate, so were not surprised by sandals and tee shirts, yet had not expected so many trees. Very few pupils made comments about the differences in colour of peoples' skin. By adding to the foreign language class the concepts of similarity and difference and by helping pupils to understand that young people in distant islands have responsibilities as young citizens just as they do, teachers were able to introduce citizenship in a **real** context. This had more impact than talking about citizenship in isolation. Being able to introduce different ethnic groups into an authentic teaching situation **and** teach in French added a very positive dimension to this cross-curricular project.

Do you know who is responsible in your school for liaison between primary and secondary schools?

• Why not suggest a cross-curricular project involving languages in next year's induction day or week for pupils moving to secondary school?

There are a number of excellent primary photo-packs of the kind described in this chapter which you can consult. For example, see *Living and learning in a Tanzanian village – a child's perspective* (Manchester Development Education Project) or *Working now* (Development Education Centre, Birmingham). While these are not designed specifically for language teaching, they can be easily adapted. See Brown, K. and Brown, M. (1998) for ways of doing this.

The potential for linking and covering several areas of the primary curriculum including foreign languages and citizenship has been demonstrated. We hope to publish this pack of materials with a teacher's guide in the future. Teachers may be happy to introduce citizenship issues **through** another subject area, or indeed through a project linking several areas, providing they have good support materials and information. Even teachers who have not visited the island of La Réunion themselves were able to suggest different topics and ideas. Delivering citizenship **without** a foreign language connection is of course possible, but the foreign language element enhances learning in other areas.

Work in progress – Morocco

Following the *La Réunion* project, we are now establishing links between a group of primary schools in York and schools in Khémisset, Morocco. A small group of teachers from both countries aim to develop materials to support the teaching of four specific areas of the curriculum: citizenship, human rights, religious education and cultural awareness through primary foreign languages. The project is being co-ordinated by Margot Brown of the Centre for Global Education and supported by Ann Gregory, Associate MFL Adviser for City of York Council, both of whom work at York St John. It has also been proposed that a parallel Initial Teacher Training project would add another dimension and assist in the expansion to other local schools. The York group visited Morocco in Autumn 2002, with a return visit by the Moroccans planned for Spring 2003. These visits will focus on exploring the culture, faith and environment of the partner country, and on collecting teaching support material and information about the country, its language teaching, culture and religious dimensions.

After the initial visits, teachers will start to develop materials and trial ways of introducing the four focus strands into the curriculum. The relative proximity of Morocco, and its popularity as a destination for UK package holidays, make visits more accessible and less expensive. Its Muslim culture, its status as a former French colony, and its rich history, as well as the varied geographical features of the country make it an attractive focus for a cross-curricular topic in Key Stage 2.

Schools in York were identified for their involvement in previous primary language development projects. It is important that schools taking part have full commitment to the project, from the Head teacher and from colleagues. If the work is to be sustainable, it needs to involve the whole school.

The *Morocco* project is still at a very early stage, but it does demonstrate how 'joined-up thinking' can operate. Projects like these will need to focus on appropriate support materials, so that any primary teacher can use them in a variety of ways. An accompanying teacher's guide, perhaps a video or CD-ROM might help. Internet sites and message boards can also support classroom teachers, and when electricity has reached pupils all over the world, multimedia and new technology will create even closer links. The resourcing of schools in Morocco is on a very different basis and this in itself provides a challenge for teachers working together.

Conclusion

By introducing fundamental concepts of citizenship in primary school, pupils can, from an early age, learn to accept and celebrate 'differences' encountered in both linguistic and cultural situations. Positive attitudes to foreign languages and to different ways of life can both be developed through an early start. For this early teaching of citizenship and language to be a success, much more contact is needed between primary and secondary teachers, to ensure continuity and progression for pupils. Good citizenship and linguistic competence both start with good communication.

Bibliography

Brown, K. and Brown, M. (1998) ResourceFile 1: *Changing places*. CILT.

Gregory, A. (2001) 'Primary foreign languages motivation' In: Chambers, G. (ed) *Reflections on motivation*. CILT.

Hawkins, E. (1981) *Modern languages in the curriculum*. Cambridge University Press.

Jones, B. (1995) Pathfinder 24: *Exploring otherness*. CILT.

Lambert, W.E. and Klineberg, O. (1967) *Children's views of foreign peoples: a cross-national survey*. New York: Appleton-Century-Crofts.

Martin, C. (2000) *An analysis of national and international research on the provision of MFL in primary schools*. QCA.

QCA (2001) *A report of the QCA project to study the feasibility of introducing a modern foreign language into the statutory curriculum at Key Stage 2*. QCA.

Schumann, J. H. (1978) *The pidginisation process. A model for second language acquisition*. Newbury House.

Tierney, D. and Hope, M (1998) Young Pathfinder 7: *Making the link: relating languages to other work in the school*. CILT.

Warwick University (2000) *An analysis and evaluation of the current situation relating to the teaching of modern foreign languages at Key Stage 2 in England*. QCA.

Useful websites

www.nacell.org.uk

www.nc.uk.net

www.standards.dfee.gov.uk

www.qca.org.uk

Chapter 7

Asylum seekers and refugees: issues for MFL teachers

Margot Brown

In this final chapter, Margot Brown looks at the experiences of asylum seekers and refugees and at ways in which all teachers, and particularly language teachers, can support them in schools. She includes practical examples of teaching activities and useful references to human rights organisations which provide support and information for people working with refugees.

Introduction

The experiences of asylum seekers and refugees raise questions of human rights which are central to citizenship education. Many people from different cultures seek refuge in this and other countries and this has implications for all teachers, including language teachers, who can respond to the need for language support, for interpreters and translators and for acceptance and positive attitudes by the receiving country. This chapter focuses on the experiences of pupils who are asylum seekers or refugees and in doing so links citizenship education and language teachers. The citizenship curriculum requires teachers to help their students develop knowledge and understanding about becoming informed citizens which includes learning about our culturally diverse society. Learning about refugees and asylum seekers, who contribute to that diversity, now, as they did in the past, is part of citizenship education. Examples and practical suggestions are given both for teachers working with children who are asylum seekers and for those teaching about these issues in the language classroom, whatever the make-up of the class.

- 14 million people are forced to seek protection in another country.

- Over 50% of asylum seekers are women and children.

- 0.47% of total asylum seekers come to UK (ratio of 1 to 972 of UK population)

- 0.15% of total asylum seekers go to Australia (ratio of 1 to 849 of Australian population)

- 17% of total asylum seekers go to Iran (ratio of 1 to 26 of Iranian population)

- 25 million people have fled their homes but not moved to another country.

- Most people seeking protection in UK in 2001 came from:
  Afghanistan – Sri Lanka – Somalia – former Yugoslavia – Iraq

- 600 unaccompanied children asylum seekers arrived in UK in 1997
  8% were granted full refugee status.
  52% were given Exceptional Leave to Remain (ELR)
  40% were refused

Sources: New Internationalist, October 2002.
iNexile; Magazine of the Refugee Council, June 2002.
Richman, N. 1998.

The context in which children of asylum seekers come to school is one where media coverage is often hostile. Young people in schools in all parts of the British Isles will be aware of the controversy surrounding their arrival. It is an important issue for schools. Some of the young people themselves will be refugees and asylum seekers who know only too well the day-to-day effects of this high-profile media coverage. No one chooses to become a refugee and many return home voluntarily once the situation in their home country improves. However, as war, internal violent conflict and oppression erupt in new areas of the world, the total number of refugees changes very little. Refugees and asylum seekers flee to many of the European countries whose languages are taught in British schools and so contribute to the cultural diversity of France, Germany, Spain and Italy to name but four. Cultural awareness for language teachers therefore will also include teaching and learning about refugee experience in European countries.

Who are refugees and asylum seekers?

The terms 'refugee' and 'asylum seeker' have distinct meanings. An asylum seeker is someone, adult or child, who has crossed an international border seeking safety in another country. Asylum seekers need to prove that they are unable to return to the country from which they have fled *owing to a well-founded fear of being persecuted for reasons of race, religion, nationality, membership of a particular social group or political opinion* (UN Convention Relating to the Status of Refugees, 1951) to be granted the legal right to remain.

A helpful starting point for teachers might be to introduce pupils to these definitions and to the Universal Declaration of Human Rights:

> *Everyone has the right to seek and to enjoy in other countries asylum from persecution. (Article 14)*

The UN produces documents relating to refugees, many of which are available in the official UN languages and on the website of the UN High Commission for Human Rights. The Council of Europe website also contains material in a range of European languages which teachers can download and use. The citizenship curriculum encourages teachers to include learning activities about the UN and the Commonwealth and this is one way of doing this.

Many refugees arrive in the UK traumatised by their experiences, terrified about their future and often unsure of their rights and entitlements. They face obstacles in the paperwork required when seeking refugee status which is often in a formal language they have difficulty understanding. While many asylum-seeking children do find school places, they may well be living with the fear of deportation. For children who arrive unaccompanied, the problems are considerably worse. The UN Convention on the Rights of the Child, which covers all young people up to the age of 18, may be a useful starting point for teachers when considering the rights of refugee and asylum-seeking children. The UK has signed this Convention and ratified it.

The Convention on the Rights of the Child specifies:

- the rights to which children are entitled and the obligation of the state to promote these rights *(Article 4)*

- the duty to provide adequate care when parents are unable to do so *(Article 3, 20)*

- the right to survival and development *(Article 6)*

- the preservation of identity *(Article 8)*

- the right to live with parents *(Article 9)*

- protection from abuse and neglect *(Article 19)*

- the right to health care *(Article 24)*

- the right to special protection for refugees and asylum seekers *(Article 22)*

- the right to benefit from Social Security *(Article 26)*

- the right to an adequate standard of living *(Article 27)*

- the right to an education that develops the child's personality and talents and respects the child's own cultural values *(Article 29)*

Richman, N. 1998: 1–2

Why are they here?

For some asylum seekers, a repressive regime which perpetrates abuses of human rights and where speaking freely can lead to detention and torture, gives grounds for flight. Belonging to the 'wrong' political party, being a member of a union or indeed trying to set one up as a way of stopping abuses can all lead to persecution. In short, most asylum seekers come to 'safe' countries because their lives are under threat in their own country.

In order to help pupils understand the nature of refugee experiences and the reasons for their flight, teachers and pupils can work on personal testimonies from asylum seekers. It is possible to find these testimonies in European languages as well as in the first languages of the asylum seekers. These can form the basis of reading analysis activities, discussion (with older students) and consideration of why European languages are spoken so frequently in other parts of the world.

Je suis dans un monde où on a peur
Et je me demande pourquoi.
Je suis dans un monde de guerre
Et je me demande pourquoi.
Je suis dans un monde avec le terrorisme
Les refugiés et le racisme
Et moi
Je me demande pourquoi.

Ils disent: ce n'est pas à une jeune fille
De poser ces grandes questions
Mais voyez le monde où on vit aujourd'hui
N'est-ce pas que j'ai raison?
Tout le monde dit non
Et moi, je me demande pourquoi.

Il y a des gens qui n'ont pas d'argent
Et je me demande pourquoi.
Les guerriers qui meurent pour leur Président
Et je me demande pourquoi.
La Terre peut vraiment mourir demain
Est-ce que le futur est dans nos mains?
Nous sommes seulement humains ...
Moi
Je me demande pourquoi.

Pupil from Gosforth High School, quoted in *MFL 1*, 2002 (CILT)

What is it like for asylum-seeking pupils in the UK?

For many new arrivals, the most important thing is a sense of security. As one Afghan girl who was resettled in Western Europe said:

> Life is: *a classroom with smiling school friends.*
> *Sunshine. A street without machine guns*
> *and a field without mines. Quiet.*
> *A home with a mother and father and*
> *brothers and sisters.*

This sense of security is vital since many will have had the trauma of seeing parents or other family members beaten or killed. They may be living with parents or other adults who are themselves traumatised and less able to support them. Schools need to be sensitive to this and teachers of all subjects alert to ways of responding.

'Although a diverse group of children, significant numbers

- have had an interrupted education in their country of origin;

- have had horrific experiences in their home countries and flight to the UK. For a small number this may affect their ability to learn and rebuild their lives;

- speak little or no English on arrival in the UK;

- suffer bullying or isolation in school;

- are not cared for by parents or usual carers, or have parents who are emotionally absent;

- are living with families who do not know their educational and social rights;

- have suffered a drop in their standard of living and other major changes in their lives.

All or any of their experiences can impede learning in the classroom.' *(Rutter, 2002)*

Experiences in the community can also affect refugee pupils' schooling. If asylum-seeking children and their families are housed in areas where there are others from the same community, there can be considerable support. Living near to those who share a common language, faith and culture, can provide a secure base from which to engage with the new, the different and the challenging. Many in the community will also have shared similar experiences in the country of origin and the flight to safety and may be able to provide an understanding ear.

However, there is a *worrying trend [which] shows clearly that asylum seekers and refugees are at real risk from racists and bullies* (Fazil Kawani, iNexile, December 2001). The reports of racial harassment to the National Asylum

Support Service (NASS) by accommodation providers and local communities include 861 incidents from May 2000 to October 2001. These include racially motivated murders.

The increase of these incidents together with the nature of much of the press and TV reporting of asylum-seeking and refugee issues make the need for work on positive responses to diversity all the more urgent. When linked with schools' duty to be proactive in combating prejudice under the Race Relations Amendment (2000) Act, it becomes all the more important to work with classes to clarify such issues. A starting point here might be the Refugee Council website and activities on press myths which can help pupils to understand the conflicting points of view which appear in the press.

Implications for language teachers

All teachers in schools have a responsibility of care for their pupils. Refugee and asylum-seeking children need that same level of care and often need additional support.

Teachers can:

- contribute to the school's induction policy to ensure the needs of refugees and asylum-seeking children are met;

- help to ensure pupils' psychological needs are met, particularly in the case of unaccompanied children;

- help to ensure that the school's anti-bullying and race equality policies actively protect refugee and asylum-seeking children from racism and bullying;

- contribute to effective home-school links;

- help to develop a 'buddy' system for refugee and asylum-seeking pupils.

Teachers of languages have particular skills and expertise to offer and they can also contribute more generally to a whole school commitment to meet the educational needs of refugee pupils.

They can find out about:

- organisations which support refugee communities including the Refugee Council; the Medical Foundation for Victims of Torture; Amnesty International-UK;

- organisations which produce materials about refugee experience such as the Minority Rights Group;

- local translation services and locally-produced information printed in a range of languages to enable entitlements to be accessed;

- Self-help guides for young refugees from the National Information Forum available in different languages.

Language teachers have a particular contribution to make in the field of language support for asylum-seeking pupils. Firstly, as discussed in the introduction, they have personal experience of learning a language and can draw on this to support pupils and their families. They can also offer support to colleagues who may not have this knowledge. Secondly, teachers of languages have experience of communicating with speakers of other languages in simple and understandable ways, without being patronising or oversimplifying their own language. They do this regularly when teaching modern foreign languages and can offer pointers for speakers of other languages when learning English. Some refugees and asylum seekers come from countries where a European language is also spoken as part of the colonial past. Zaïre would be one such example. Teachers who speak the relevant European language can be of enormous help in settling young asylum-seeking pupils into a new and often challenging environment.

While some children will speak or understand a European language other than English, many will not. Supporting these young people linguistically, to enable them to take part in the life of the school, is of particular importance. Teachers of languages can offer very specific support to children and families alike. While it is important to learn English to participate fully in school and community life, a pupil's first language is also an important part of her cultural identity. Some asylum-seeking children (such as Turkish Kurds) may already have had their first language prohibited by oppressive regimes. It is important to maintain the first language of asylum-seeking children so that they can continue to communicate with all their family members and so that they can settle back into their home community should they return. For many refugees this is a great hope.

However, while supporting first languages can be problematic for schools due to lack of adequate funding, supplementary schools can be of enormous benefit for all.

> Supplementary schools, in which reading and writing in the first language are taught, are very important in maintaining first language literacy. This does not interfere with English. Contrary to what one might expect, research (among others Cummins, 1984; Edwards, 1998) shows that developing first language skills and doing some school work in their own language promotes overall capacities to think and learn. This is related to the ease with which complex ideas and new concepts can be developed in the first language.

> Some children are not motivated to keep up or learn skills in their own language. They resent having to spend extra time in supplementary school especially if the lessons are formal, but it is important to encourage first language learning.
> (Richman, 1998: 36)

Teaching about refugee and asylum-seeking issues in the MFL classroom

The potential of MFL to contribute to the citizenship curriculum was discussed in the opening chapter. In addition to the QCA Schemes of Work an increasing number of resources support MFL teaching of citizenship. Some of these include information and activities to help pupils understand the experiences of refugee and asylum-seeking children and provide an important balance to press reports which are often misinformed and tend to demonise asylum-seeking families.

Recent research found that

> *Many of the refugee students in the secondary schools studied were subjected to prejudice and discrimination. ... Among many of the non-refugee pupils interviewed there was superficial acceptance of refugee pupils but underneath there was quite a lot of hostility, some outright racism and a considerable amount of wearied acceptance on both sides.*
> (Jones, 1998: 178)

Teaching about the refugee experience not only contributes to the citizenship curriculum but also to the school's work in response to the Race Relations Amendment Act and to recommendations for schools made in the Macpherson Report (the Stephen Lawrence Inquiry), which Ofsted has a responsibility to monitor. Recent publications for Amnesty International (2002) by the Education in Human Rights Network and the Centre for Global Education include handbooks for teachers of French and Spanish. The Minority Rights Group has produced the 'Voices' series which contains a collection of extracts from interviews with refugees from Zaïre; Angola; Sudan and Uganda.

Les conflits au Zaïre

Nous devions quitter le Zaïre parce que la situation devenait très dangereuse. Mon papa craignait que nous soyions tués. Presque tous les jours il y avait des troubles dans les villes et les villages. Les gens se battaient dans les magasins pour voler de la nourriture et de l'argent. Les soldats volaient et quand ils sont venus dans notre école ils ont blessé un enseignant à coups de couteau parce qu'il avait refusé de leur donner de l'argent. J'avais horreur de voir des gens blessés et étendus morts. Je suis si heureux d'être en Angleterre parce qu'on ne se bat pas ici.

Ecrit par un garçon de 9 ans, élève à l'école primaire de Enfield, Middlesex. Ceci est un récit oral fait à son maître.

Source: *Voices from Zaïre* (1995) Minority Rights Group.

What activity could you develop to extend your pupils' understanding?

Many of the organisations which work with refugees have an education officer who, in addition to supporting refugee children in school, also works with schools with no refugee population on ways of teaching about refugees. This standard activity could be readily adapted for the languages classroom:

You've got 10 minutes to get out

What would you take that could save your life?

If you were one of the world's 15 million refugees, you'd need some survival tips. Death threats or violent encounters with local security forces will have probably made you fear for your life. Take a few minutes to calm yourself, then, if you're not already at home, get there, get packed and get out.

- **Mementos**
  Family snap shots may not seem like a priority when the police or army want to gun you down, but you may never see your loved ones again. Photographs are easily carried but if folded or allowed to get wet, they easily perish.

- **Cooking implements**
  Most refugees have no idea how long they will be on the road. If you are cold, or if you are supplied with raw cereal rations from aid agencies, you will need an old can or biscuit box in which to cook.

- **Tools**
  For many refugees, a knife is the most basic tool.

- **Water**
  If you're fleeing within central Africa, you're going to need at least two litres every day. There are wells and water supplies in some villages – try to get hold of a bottle or can.

- **Blankets**
  If you're a Kurd fleeing Iraqi death squads, you're probably headed to the mountains in south-east Turkey. Night-time temperatures can drop to -20°C or lower. This is cold enough to kill a fit person in one night.

- **Food**
  You may be able to scavenge on the road but in war zones, this is highly dangerous. Do not weigh yourself down with supplies.

- **Shoes**
  Most refugees travel on foot. If you don't have adequate protection for your feet, you will have cuts and blisters. In hot climates, wounds become a breeding ground for maggots and other parasites. Old tyre tread is easily cut for replacement sandal soles.

Many people endure years of persecution before they finally leave behind everything they've ever owned. The ones who get out fast are the lucky ones. In 1948, the Universal Declaration of Human Rights stated that anyone in fear of persecution should be able to seek a safe refuge. It is a very basic human right. We'd like to remind every government in the world of that. And to say that closing doors on refugees is simply sending people back to meet their fate.

Amnesty International

School students rarely think to pack passports (if they have one) or evidence that supports their view of the danger they are in. This is also a problem for real refugees and asylum seekers.

Conclusion

We identified, in the opening chapter of this book, the importance of acknowledging cultural diversity in definitions of citizenship. Language teachers are well placed to help pupils learn about and understand diversity in the United Kingdom and to develop an awareness of cultural diversity in the countries which speak the language they are learning. By using refugee testimonies, through role-play and the consideration of information and statistics drawn from the world-wide web, pupils develop knowledge and understanding and skills which contribute to their development as citizens of the increasingly culturally diverse world in which we all live.

Bibliography

Brown, M. (ed) (2002) *Human rights in the curriculum; French*. Amnesty International.

Brown, M. (ed) (2002) *Human rights in the curriculum; Spanish*. Amnesty International.

Cummins (1984) *Bilingualism and special education*. Multilingual Matters.

Donnellan, C. (ed) (1999) *Refugees and asylum seekers*. Independence Publishers.

Edwards, V. (1998) *The power of Babel – teaching and learning in multilingual classrooms*. Trentham Books.

iNexile, *Magazine of the refugee council*, June 2002.

Jones, C. (1998) '*The educational needs of refugee children*' In: Rutter, J. and Jones, C. (eds) *Refugee education, mapping the field*. Trentham Books.

Minority Rights Group (MRG) (1998) *Forging new identities – young refugees and minority students tell their stories*, Minority Rights Group.

National Information Forum (2001) *How to make a new life in the UK: a self-help guide for young refugees and asylum seekers* (available in many languages, including French, Arabic and English) National Information Forum.

New Internationalist No. 350, October 2002, '*The case for open borders*'.

Richman, N. (1998) *In the midst of the whirlwind – a manual for helping refugee children*. Trentham Books.

Rutter, J. and Jones, C. (1998) *Refugee Education; mapping the field*. Trentham Books.

Rutter, J. (2002) *Asylum seekers and refugees, modern language teachers and citizenship education* (available from the author, London Metropolitan University)

Warner, R. (ed) (1995) *Voices from Sudan*, London, MRG. *Voices from Zaïre*, MRG (part of the African Voices Series).

Useful websites

Websites from UNHCR **www.unhcr.ch** and the Council of Europe **www.coe.int** provide their information in all the main languages. Try also **www.hcrfrance.org.**

www.refugeecouncil.org.uk

Contributors

Jim Anderson is Lecturer in Modern Languages in Education at Goldsmiths' College, University of London. He has a particular interest in bilingualism and is a member of the CILT Advisory Group for Community Languages. A current research interest is the potential of ICT in enhancing the learning and teaching of community languages.

Kim Brown was a secondary languages teacher in Warwickshire before moving into teacher education in 1990. She worked at the University of East Anglia for five years and is currently conducting a longitudinal research project into the lives and careers of the language teachers she trained while she was there.

Margot Brown is the national co-ordinator of the Centre for Global Education, York St John College, York. She is currently working in human rights education and has worked with teachers of languages to publish human rights materials for French and Spanish classes. She is a trainer and works with colleagues at the Centre to provide CPD courses.

Margaret Burr is the Co-ordinator of the Humanities Education Centre. As part of a network of Development Education Centres, HEC aims to promote the values and principles of development education and global citizenship enabling people to understand the links between their own lives and those of people throughout the world.

Michael Byram is Professor of Education at the University of Durham, England. Since being appointed to a post in teacher education at the University of Durham in 1980, he has carried out research into the education of linguistic minorities and foreign language education, and is now Director of Research Degrees at Durham University. He is a Special Adviser to the Council of Europe Language Policy Division, and is currently interested in language education policy and the politics of language teaching.

Manju Chaudhuri is a freelance consultant in the area of community languages. She has long experience of teaching Bengali and EAL and has also worked as a co-ordinator for Bengali and community languages in the London Borough of Tower Hamlets. Her previous publications include a wide range of materials to support the teaching of Bengali.

Therese Comfort is Advanced Skills Teacher and class teacher at Headlands Primary School, Haxby, York. She has been involved in teaching languages to KS2 pupils for over ten years and is particularly interested in integrating Modern Foreign Languages into other areas of the KS2 curriculum.

Ian Davies et al. **Ian Davies** is based at the University of York, UK. **Peter Cunningham** at London Metropolitan University, UK. **Mark Evans** at the Ontario Institute for Studies in Education, University of Toronto, Canada. **Gunilla Fredriksson** at Linköping University, Sweden. **Graham Pike** at the University of Prince Edward Island, Canada. **Hanns-Fred Rathenow** and **Felicitas Tesch** at the Technical University of Berlin, Germany. **Alan Sears** is based at the University of New Brusnwick, Canada. We are collaborating on a project for citizenship education and initial teacher education that is funded by the European Commission and the Canadian Government.

Ann Gregory is a Senior Lecturer at York St John College and acts as Associate MFL Adviser to the City of York Council. She has taught languages in schools and higher education and is involved in teacher training, In Service support, consultancy and Lingua projects centred on primary MFL. She is particularly interested in using the foreign language to strengthen links with other areas of the curriculum.

Sally Hicks is Deputy Head at Fulford Cross School in York. She has taught in mainstream and special schools and has a particular interest in the teaching of languages within a global context.

Audrey Osler is Director of the Centre for Citizenship Studies in Education at the University of Leicester. Her research interests address issues of human rights, equality and identity. Her recent books include *Girls and exclusion: rethinking the agenda* (Routledge Falmer, 2003, with Kerry Vincent) and *Citizenship and democracy in schools' diversity, identity, equality* (Trentham, 2000)

Hugh Starkey is Senior Lecturer in the School of Education at the University of Leicester. He is responsible for the postgraduate teacher education course in Citizenship and researches issues of education for democracy and human rights within the Centre for Citizenship Studies in Education.